# THE MAKING OF AN EXPERT ENGINEER

Chief Editor of Book
**Mr. Abhishek Bansal**

Editor of Book
Dr. S.K. Singh

Editor of Book
Dr. Gaurav

ANJUMAN
PRAKASHAN

Title : The Making of an Expert Engineer
Chief Editor of Book : Mr. Abhishek Bansal,
Editor of Book : Dr. S.K. Singh,
Editor of Book : Dr. Gaurav

Published By-
**Anjuman Prakashan**
942, Mutthiganj, Prayagraj, 211003
www.anjumanpublication.com
anjumanprakashan@gmail.com

Printed and bound in India
Paperback, First published by Anjuman Prakashan in 2022
ISBN : 978-93-91531-44-7
Copyright © 2022 All Authors of Book
Printing rights reserved : Anjuman Prakashan 2022
Cover & Typeset by Anjuman Prakashan

Price in india: 250.00

**Dedication**

Jind Institute of Engineering & Technology,
Jind (126102), Haryana

# PREFACE

Dear readers 'The Making of an Expert Engineer' is a specialized book which will tell you the quality of perfect engineer and how these quality can be enhanced. As we know this is the time of ultra specialization. This book contains eighteen chapters which cover most of the aspect of an engineer's life.

The subject matter of present work has emerged from various readings and experience which the authors have accumulated over the years of teaching students. Keeping in view the present needs for an expert engineer, this book provides a holistic view of what an expert engineer should be and how the related characteristics can be obtained. It covers conceptual, financial, legal, statistical, technical, as well as ethical aspects of an engineer's life which will enhance the knowledge, skills and attitude of an engineer. This book has been written in a very simple language, with clear idea and containing logical ways of expression.

We would welcome the comments and suggestions by the readers for further improvement of the book.

# CONTENT

# RECENT CHALLENGES IN ELECTRICAL ENGINEERING: FOR MAKING AN EXPERT ENGINEER IN PRESENT SCENARIO.

Author : Amanjyoti Sethi,
Assistant Professor,
Department of Electrical Engineering,
Jind Institute of Engineering and Technology, Jind (126102), Haryan.

## ABSTRACT

Electrical engineering is a wide area starting from electricalpower generation to distribution to end users. Due to many devices present in electrical system it has become complex to understand and control, but these devices have many benefits .Computer engineering is an amalgam of several fields of engineering like electrical and computers, which focuses on programming and integration with hardware devices. Electrical engineering is always a challenging field which requires consistency with proper control and communication system.  The main challenges in electrical power system are increasing demand, malwares, power electronic technology trends etc.

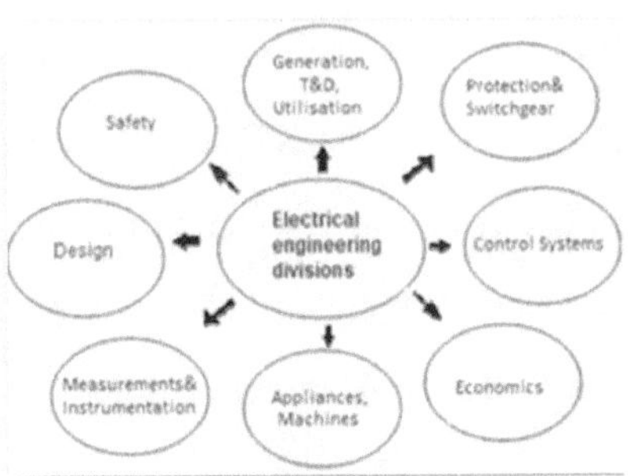


**Figure-1**

## INTRODUCTION

Electrical engineering is a wide field which consists of Power Generation, Transmission, Distribution, Protection, Switchgear and we use these devices through conversion and measurement .The schematic diagram of all these divisions is shown in Fig. 1. In early days the main function of transmission and distribution system I how to send power at sending end through mechanical modes. But with the development of new techniques and with the help of power electronics devices we can ensure that our system is controlled both at sending end and receiving end .With the help of IT sector , regular up gradation  and power electronics trends our power system becomes automated and reliable . Also the new techniques like FACTS (Flexible Alternating Current Transmission System) and High Voltage Direct Current Transmission System (HVDC) has made the power system more efficient. But there are some risks which challenges the durability of electrical engineering and its constituents

However we can control our system by using power electronics devices and for fast communication we  use various types of network like LAN (Local Area Network), NAN (Neighborhood Area Network), WAN (Wide Area Network) and HAN (Home Area Network) etc. which make easy to eliminate risks .But the main drawback of this IT sector which we use in our electrical engineering system is attacked by various types of malwares and viruses .At the same time IT with computers are playing a vital role in operation and management of electrical power system network.

## II.RECENT CHALLENGES IN POWER SYSTEM

According to the World Energy Council's the demand of electrical energy by 2040 is 50 PWh (Peta Watt hours) which is double to that in the year 2007 so our main challenge is how to match supply and demand in a safe and reliable way. To meet the demand with safe, secure and reliable power there are many challenges which arise from sending end to receiving which we will discuss briefly

### A. GENERATION

"The rate of depletion of natural resources like oil and coal raises serious concerns about feasibility and reliability. We can use renewable sources as alternate like wind energy, solar energy, bio energy which ensures sustainable development and we can also conserve non-conventional source of energy. Also, the evolution of Distributed Generation (DG) at user level and de-regulated generation models also cause a major change in power generation sector. Implementation of these new models to the exiting power system involves several challenges like stability, synchronization, fault currents and harmonics due to Power Electronic Devices (PED). And to maintain such a complex and hybrid system, there is a need of highly developed software technology that can detect and maintain these systems efficiently."

### B. Transmission And Distribution

The demand of renewable source of energy is increasing day by day due this the complexity at sending end and at receiving end also increased and in addition to frequently changes in load due to various types of new load like chargeable vehicles ,smart phones, portable devices and other non linear load increase the difficulty on transmission and distribution system . Also, the de-regulated power transmission and distribution models rapidly increase the complexity of power system. These problems need advanced technical solutions like power electronics trends, smart grids, FACTS

## C. Utilization

Due to the presence of various consumers in the usage of electricity and availability of various gadgets like smart phones, TV, electronics devices used in kitchen the demand of reliable and uninterrupted supply will also increase. The major challenge is to predict the load and arrangement of that load without much disturbance to the consumer there is also a lot of initiation by local authorities to generate and utilize the electrical energy locally, like solar power plant, with an alternate option of transmits surplus energy back to the grid. This system requires checking over a period of time, two-way metering and two-way communication systems... The chance of cyber -attacks can also be increased by using various smart gadgets like television, microwave, electric vehicles, charging devices communicate with remote controllers by using internet and mobile apps. To mitigate these problems our monitoring system should be strict.

## D. Switchgear And Protection

Due to the presence of new devices and new models nowadays

the fault current in the transmission and distribution system increases as compare to the traditional generation system .There is maloperation of protective relays due to presence of these fault current and will endanger the other protective devices The cause of such faults currents occur due to several reasons afor example the earth fault current occur at any solar integrated grid will contribute the current not only at distribution side but also at generation side that is at generation side . Due to  excess use of power generating sources the monitoring of fault current becomes difficult. For the better stability our complex grid requires fast solution like to isolate fault circuits digital relays run on simple software system and we can protect the system by simply giving command to trip the circuit breaker. But the use of Information Technology (IT) and modern communication tools create new problems like malwares and cyber-attacks which are to be addressed properly. But the use of software's and various types of communication tools used in our electrical power system will create new problems like cyber -attacks and software's

## THREATS AND OPPORTUNITIES AT PRESENT SCENARIO

In India our grid system is highly wide which is made by human like any other system so it has both threats and opportunities which we will discuss below

### A. Threats

Various confront face  by electrical power system are grid stability, environmental conditions, man-made threats, virus -attacks, mismatch between supply and demand , disynronzation between various generation facilities, regulatory obligations, depleted natural resources, non availability of skilled manpower, huge investments, political changes, technological obsolescence and changes, system resilience and so on. To come out of these problems and to grab the opportunities available, electrical engineering is moving towards smart systems with the help of IT, Power electronics and Computers.

### B. Opportunities

"The technological advancements in electrical, electronics, computer and communications engineering supporting the global leaders aim of de-carbonized and green power system. The developments and opportunities took place so far and the ongoing solutions are discussed in subsequent sections. By using PED, which has built-in self supervision facility? The overall availability up to 99% can be achieved. B.1 Smart Grids (SG) The definition of SG per The European Technology Platform, "It is an electricity network that can indigently integrate the actions of all users connected to it-generators, consumers and those that do both – in order to efficiently deliver sustainable, economic and secure electricity suppliers" It is an electrical grid which consists of conventional& renewable energy resource, smart appliances, smart meters etc. with two-way communication, whose schematic is shown in Fig. 2. It has re-engineered the electrical utility divisions with the use of power electronic conditioning & communication devices for smooth conditioning and control." These words are said by jean Claude

"B.1 Smart Grids (SG) The definition of SG per The European Technology Platform, "It is an electricity network that can indigently integrate the actions of all users connected to it-generators, consumers and those that do both – in order to efficiently deliver sustainable, economic and secure electricity suppliers" It is an electrical grid which consists of conventional& renewable energy resource, smart appliances, smart meters etc. with two-way communication, whose schematic is shown in Fig. 3. It has re-engineered the electrical utility divisions with the use of power electronic conditioning & communication devices for smooth conditioning and control." This words are said by Neil kato

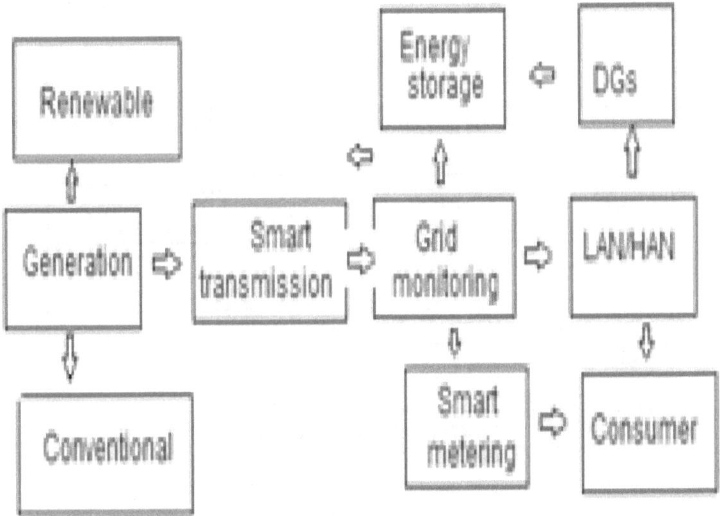


**Figure-2**

Figure-3 shows about the one way of power grid system which is essential part of power production.

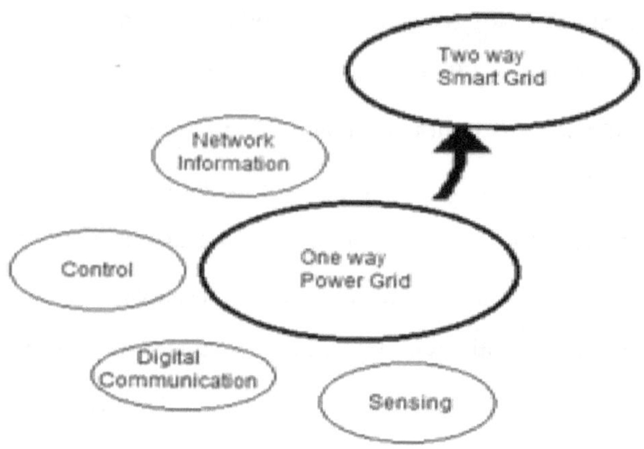


**Figure-3**

**Difference between Present Conventional Grid and Future**

**Smart Grid**

| Present Conventional Grid | Future Smart Grid |
|---|---|
| Electro-mechanical | Digital |
| One-way communication | Two-way communication |
| Centralized generation | Distributed generation |
| Few or sensor less | Throughout sensors |
| Manual monitoring | Self-monitoring |
| Manual restoration | Self-healing |
| Failures and blackouts | Adaptive islanding |
| Limited control | Full control |
| Limited customer choices | Many customer choices |

**Table-1**

MICRO-GRIDS *(MG):*

Itisalocalminipowergridwhichcanoperateasaseparate small entity or in collaboration with other small grids. The schematic diagram is shown in Fig. 4, whose scope is generally to have its own local generation and storage facilities with a pre-decided zone restriction.

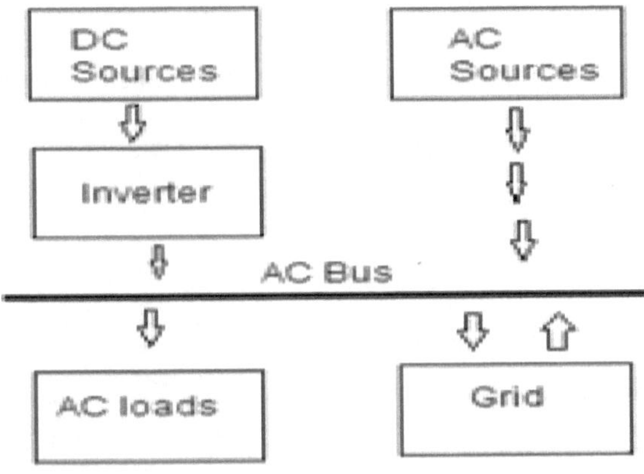


**Figure-4**

## DISTRIBUTED GENERATION (DG):

The benefits of de-centralized and new generating stations are having storage facilities and close to load centers. The diagram of this shown in Fig. 5

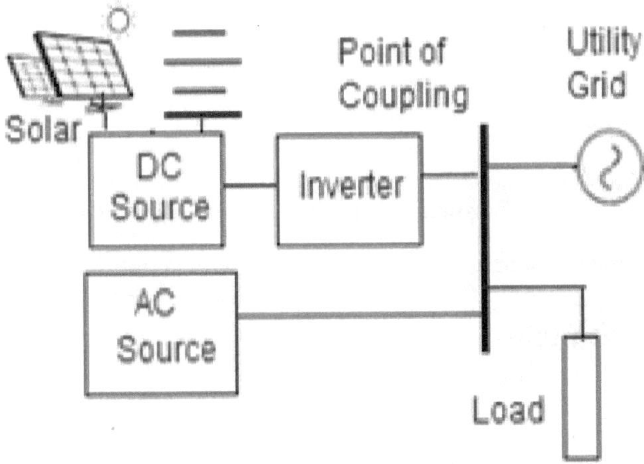


**Figure-5**

They use of  small Hydroelectric power plants, Turbine generators, Solar power plants, Biomass, Wind power and Geothermal power units and serves loads up to 10MW and also being used for power back  ups, as shown in Fig. 6.

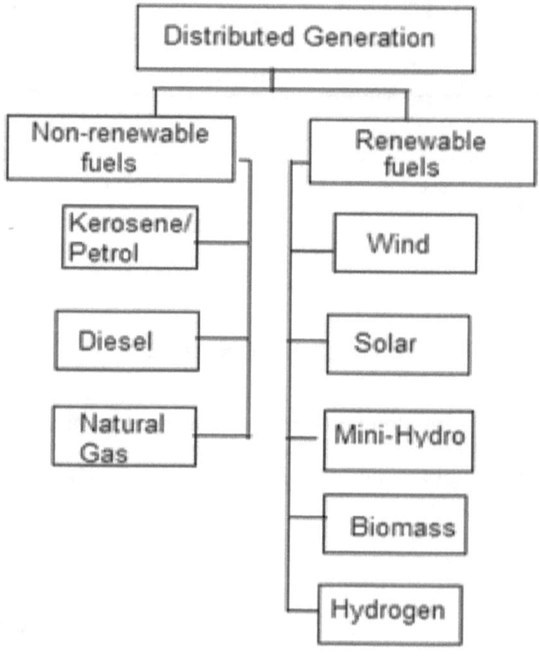


**Figure-6**

They can be coordinated with in a SG and have the opportunity to protect environment and improves continuity of supply.

**CONCLUSION**

We can save time, efforts, energy and other resource by implementing the IT software and technology in power production sector.

# PRINCIPLES OF PRODUCTION ENGINEERING

Author : Ashish Singla
Registrar,
Department of Administration,
Jind Institute of Engineering and Technology, Jind (126102), Haryana.

Production Engineering is the specialized knowledge that helps in designing, researching, developing, implementing, and controlling a product. Production engineering is the process of converting any product from raw material to finished good. This is the only technology that makes the product safe and effective. Different types of products are made in different industries in a production engineering process. Before producing a product, it has a long planning in which what to produce, its quality, quantity, price, size, color, demand and supply is analyzed. Production engineer is responsible for productively related planning, manufacturing, inspection, development, management, controlling, directing. The production engineer is responsible for the testing, improvement and safety of a product after it is ready.

Some Skills of a Production Engineer:-

1) **Communication Skill**

2) **Problem Solving**

3) **Teambuilding**

4) **Leadership**

5) **Technical Skill**

6) **Locus on Control**

7) **Sigma**

8) **Decision Making**

9) **Competitive Skill**

**(1). Communication Skill: -**Communication is the backbone of a business organization. Communication is the transmission of information, acts, ideas and thoughts from one person to another. Communication in an organization helps in sending a business idea and related information to other people, So that people do their work in the right way and in the best way. In a communication process, communication can take place in any style, such as verbal and nonverbal. Communication helps in directing the employees and this process ends with the feedback.

**(2). Problem Solving:-**Problem solving techniques is most important for a production engineer. A production team has to face many difficulties in doing production, it's not easy to understand and solve these problems. Special knowledge is needed to solve the problem and then only these problems can be solved. To solve the problems, a long planning has to be done and the strategy is made keeping the future problems in mind. The steps for solving problems are as follows:-

- **Define the type of problem**

- **Find the alternatives**

- **Evaluate alternatives**

- **Find best alternatives**

- **Implementation**

- **Evaluate the results**

**(3). Teambuilding:** -Team building is a process in which many people are gathered together to work together. This is an activity in which all the people are taken together and the work is distributed among them. A manager turns peoples into a team to fulfill the company's objectives, helping them meet the needs of an organization. Some team building skills are as follows:-

- **Delegation**

- **Motivation**

- **Communication**

- **Collaboration**

- **Problem Solving**

- **Accountability**

**(4). Leadership:** -A leader is a person who can lead a team or group, assist in the production process, and effectively deal with the challenges ahead. A leader is a team player who leads his team as well as provides his team with an environment where an industrial team can work with satisfaction. A leader is also a good manager, communicator, and motivator who always keep on motivating his team. Some qualities of a leader:-

- **Positive Thinker**

- **Reliable**

- **Time Effective**

- **Flexible**

- **Risk Taker**

- **Decision Maker**

**(5). Technical Skill:-**A production manager should always be a technical minded person. He should be aware of technical change because technology is a rapidly changing thing. He should also have full knowledge of it. Any decision should be taken by looking at the technology at the time of production; technology can directly affect the production decision.

**(6). Locus on Control**:-Locus of control is an important technique of a business organization. Locus of control means complete control from the focal point of the business to the external elements as well. A production process is influenced by many decisions and factors. Making decisions according to the situation is the hallmark of a good production head. It can only do that which can control the whole system. Therefore it is important that an engineer should also be proficient in locus of control.

**(7). Sigma:** -A Production Engineer should also be familiar with Sigma concepts. Sigma means improving the quality, quantity, color, appearance, size of a product within a production process and minimizing the cost and profit maximization in the production process. Along with providing quality products to the customers, Sigma also includes improving their requirement and employees' morale. Some types of sigma are as follows:-

- **Statistics**

- **Process management**

- **Continuous improvement**

- **Quality Culture**

**(8). Decision Making:** -Decision making is the most important part of the production process. During production, many decisions have to be taken day to day, ranging from planning, directing, controlling, strategic decision, product quality, time management, service and cost related decisions. Apart from this, decisions related to customer related development, customer satisfaction, waste management, services and maintenance of machines and technology are also taken. That's why a production engineer should be a decision maker as well as a decision maker.

**(9). Competitive Skill:** -Competitive skill refers to the skill that puts an organization ahead of its competitors. A good production engineer can become a good competitor only when he has complete knowledge of the market and his competitors. For this he should have complete knowledge of SWOT .SWOT roles aid important in competitive skills. SWOT meaning is:-

- **S – Strength**
- **W – Weakness**
- **O– Opportunities**
- **T- Threat**

**Types of Factors in Production**

Some factors that play an important role in production are as follows:-

1. **Land**
2. **Labor**
3. **Capital**
4. **Entrepreneur**

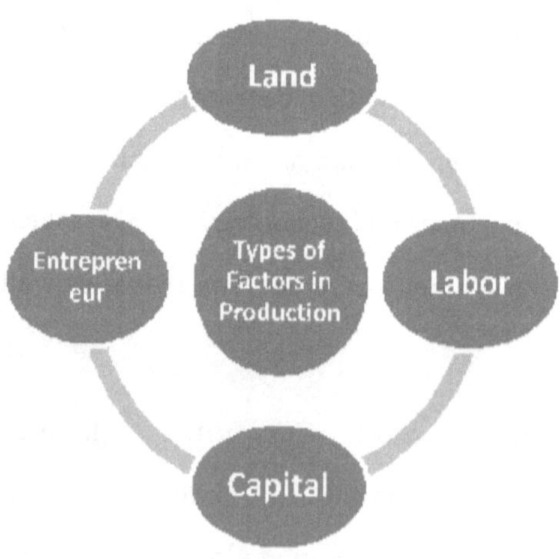


**Types of Factors in Production**

**(1). Land:** -Land is the first and most important part of production factors, providing a direction to our production system. Here is such a natural resource that provides us with a basis for production as well as for our living. Land is a fixed asset as well as a gift from God to a man. Land is in different forms in different business. Land is a piece in the production industry that creates a place for production according to the requirements of the production. The selection of land is done considering the area around it such as air, water, soil and other natural resources. The selection of land should be according to the transportation and market area, otherwise the production of the product or the company may fail. Some of the land types are Agriculture land, Industrial land, Residential land, Educational land etc.Some characteristics of a land:-

- **God Gift to Man**

- **Natural Resource**

- **Immovable**

- **Fixed Asset**

- **Multi Use**

**(2). Labor:-**Labor means doing any physical and mental work by a human being. In which a man is paid something in return for his service. Labor plays an important role in producing a product. Hard working labor is usually only unskilled labor, which does physical work. The one who does mental work is a professional labor who has knowledge of a particular area such as doctors, engineers, teachers, advocates and officers in different areas. They also play an important role in the production process; they help in the preparation of any product from processing to finished good. Some Types of labors:-

- **Skilled Labor**

- **Unskilled labor**

- **Mental Labor**

- **Physical Labor**

**(3). Capital:-**Capital does not mean only money which we need for production like land, building, machinery and those things which are important for production. Rather, capital also refers to the human workforce that assists in production as well as from making a product to its final consumer also reaches. Thus capital means land, building, machinery, material and the workforce that helps us in production. Some different types of capital:-

- **Financial Capital**

- **Natural Resources**

- **Human Resources**

- **Social Capital**

**(4).Entrepreneur:-**Entrepreneur is a professional person who collects all the resources of production, invests money in business, invents new ideas and bears the risks. An Entrepreneur organizes, manages, directs and controls the activities of a businessman Entrepreneur also possesses Technical Skills, Problem Solving Skills, Risk Taking, Flexibility and Analytical Skills. Some Successful entrepreneurs:-

- **Bill Gates - Microsoft**

- **Steve Jobs - Apple**

- **Ritesh Agarwal - OYO**

- **Mark Zuckerberg – Facebook**

- **Jeff Bezos - Amazon**

- **R.K. Rowlings - Harry Potter**

- **Jahangir Ratanji Dadabhoy Tata  - Tata Group**

- **Lakshmi Niwas Mittal - Arcelor**

- **Azim Premji - Wipro**

**Factors Affecting of Production**

Many decisions are taken in a business related to running the business; they are influenced by many factors which can be both internal and external. Many factors give rise to production, these include both internal factor and external factor. Some trends are like this:-

**(1). Internal Factors**

**(2). External Factors**

**(1). Internal Factors:** -Instead of internal factors, those factors which start with the planning of a business and which influence the decisions within the business.

a) **Communication:** -Communication is an important part in business; it is done randomly before taking any decision. It is seen inside that whether any decision has been properly conveyed or not. Many barriers come in the poet of any information such as Language Barrier, Physical Barrier, Organizational Barrier, Emotional Barrier etc. Therefore it is necessary that these barriers should be removed and further communication should be made to the employees properly.

b) **Infrastructure:** -No work can be done without infrastructure support, what kind of infrastructure is the place where a project is being set up. A project engineer should analyze the local situation before production, how is the land there, transport facility, lighting support, availability of raw mall is correct or not. Then it would be right to take a decision.

c) **Finance:** -Finance is the most important requirement of any business. Without it no business can run. Hence fund requirement is always important. Finance decision for a business is very important. For this a project head should find those houses which can meet the requirement of the fund. For this, the help of financial institution can be taken which can fulfill this deficiency of ours and can come and meet the means of day by day needs.

d) **Coordination:** -Coordination is a very important thing in any organization, which helps employees to work as well as increases motivation. It is the responsibility of a production engineer to maintain trust among the employees so that there is a harmonious relation between them. A satisfied employee helps in maximum production.

**e) Production Planning:** -Production planning is as essential for an organization as it is to go from production to product. Under production planning, a strategy is made of the process from the design of a product to the completion of the product. This decision is made keeping in mind the market survey and customer needs. In this, the product's design, color, size, cost, material, and the material used in it are also analyzed. After the product is ready, it also includes testing it.

**f) Raw Material:** -Raw material is as much a resource in any production line as the presence of blood in the body. Raw material refers to the material which is used in the production to prepare a new product such as cloth from cotton; sugar from sugarcane etc.Converting a raw material into a finished material takes a long process and time-consuming planning. In this, along with waste management and time management, cost is also taken care of.

**g) Machinery:** -Machinery is such an important part of any production line that helps the raw material to reach the finished good. Different types of machinery are used in different production lines like electronic, electrical, mechanical etc.Machinery can be in any foam such as transport, production machinery, any device etc.It is necessary to take care of them from time to time and it is necessary to change them according to time, otherwise it can cause great harm to the production.

**(2). External Factors:** -Like the internal environment, the study of the external environment is also very important; it also affects the production in the same way as the internal factors. For these also it is necessary to make a right strategy like for internal factors.

**a) Social Environment:-**The social environment is one of the most important factors in a business organization. This includes our customers, suppliers and our society where our business is set up. If we do not do market audit properly, then it can make a huge loss to our business, before making production in it, we should do market survey by making the right strategy.

**b) Political environment: -**Political environment includes all the rules and regulations that the government sets for a business organization. These rules and regulations directly affect any business, if a business does any work in an illegal way, then the government can impose heavy fine on it as well as ban it. It is the responsibility of any business that no one should do any such work that they have to face such a situation. Apart from this, if any business is with our enemy country, then if a war situation is created, then the government can make it too. That's why any business should keep all these things in mind.

**c) Cultural Environment: -**Cultural environment refers to the environment in which people are associated with one culture, they have different beliefs, different people follow different cultures. In which different people believe in different ideologies and different traditions, due to which a production engineer should produce everything keeping the culture in mind. Like there is a different culture in foreign countries and India's culture is different.

**d) Technical Environment:** - Technological Change is an Uncertain Thing; new and new technologies keep coming in the market, it is very important to be aware of them. Knowledge of technology proves effective in making a good technical strategy. Old technology puts a negative impact on the production system, so it is important to stay updated with new technology and keep making technical changes.Nokia has a great example of this which proves how important technical changes are. Knowledge of technology makes us ahead of our competitors.

**e) International Environment:-**When a business crosses the borders of one country and establishes in another country, it has to behave accordingly. In an international business, a business has to face the rules and regulations of the government in another country, a business cannot disobey these rules and regulations even if it wants. Apart from these, a business also has to face its culture, social, technical, natural environment. The customer also directly influences a business, his choice; product size and cost also matter. Therefore, after understanding all these things in detail, any production should be established.

**f) Natural Environment:** -It is very important to study the natural environment because the natural environment directly affects our business. It is very important to be aware of natural disasters; it is like an uninvited guest. This spinach can destroy our manufacturing unit in the blink of an eye. Such as earthquakes, tsunamis or cyclones in sea areas and avalanches in the mountains and mountain slopes are very difficult to predict. Therefore, the production line should be established only after their detailed study.

**Conclusion:-**

Production is the first need of any organization that helps a business grows. The imagination of any business cannot be without production, it is necessary to study the entire internal and external environment inside it. These things also affect the production badly. Production planning and environment study should be done with great care; even a small lack of it can affect a large business line. All the factors that happen play an important role in this whether it is land, capital, labor or entrepreneur. All these factors give success to any business and if they are not selected properly, they can affect the production process and hinder the fulfillment of the company's objectives.

**References**


- https://www.toppr.com/guides/business-economics/theory-of-production-and-cost/factors-of-production-land/

- https://www.economicsdiscussion.net/labour/labour-meaning-kinds-and-importance-economics/13749

- https://www.tutorialspoint.com/international_business_management/country_attractiveness.htm

# RESEARCH METHODS FOR BUSINESS: A SKILL-BUILDING APPROACH BOOK REVIEW FOR THE MAKING OF AN EXPERT ENGINEER.

Reviewed By: Dr. Gaurav,
Assistant Professor,
Department of Management Studies,
Jind Institute of Engineering and Technology, Jind (126102) (Haryana).

**Title:** Research Methods for Business: A Skill-Building Approach.

**Author:** Uma Sekaran and Roger Bougie

**Publisher:** Wiley India Pvt. Ltd.

**Year:** 2016, 6th Edition

**ISBN:** 978-81-265-5674-8

## RESEARCH METHODS FOR BUSINESS: A SKILL-BUILDING APPROACH.

Research Methods for Business: A Skill-Building Approach is a reference book for business research which provides practical perspectives on how research can be done and applied in real business situations. It contains 423 pages and seventeen chapters, but it is an ocean in a pot. Maintaining Uma Sekaran' s popular and accessible style of writing, Roger Bougie draws upon his extensive experience in the field to present an up-to-date guide on business research which is ideal for aspiring managers and research scholars. The sixth edition has been fully revised and updated to include cutting-edge examples and rich pedagogical features designed to improve students and managers learning outcomes. There is now an increased emphasis on the relationship between the scientific and the pragmatic approaches to research, while the key concepts are explored and applied to real-life research throughout the book.

First chapter of the book elaborates the research. It contains so many definitions about research. One of them is, a research is organized, systematic, data based, critical objective, inquiry of investigation for a specific problem. It helps in creating the better criteria for making decision. In the second chapter scientific approaches and alternative approaches are discussed. Which helps a researcher to set role and models of research. It also contains does and don't in research. In the third chapter research process and problem formulation techniques are given. According to the author it is first step of research because, to identify the problem, is a foundation of research. The fourth chapter is about the literature review, its role and functions. It also contains different techniques to write the references. The fifth chapter is about the formulation of hypothesis, its kind and process. Here some variables are also discussed which effects on research like dependent vs independent and moderating vs mediating. The sixth chapter is about the elements of research design. Different types of research design like exploratory, descriptive and casual studies are also discussed. A criterion for good research is also discussed into a sensitive manner. In the seventh chapter, data, classification of data, methods of data collection and sources of information discussed. Special focus is given on interview, as interview is better technique for collection of data. The eight chapter has explained observation, as a tool for collection of data. Because observation is a field watching process and can give a better data for research. It also contains different techniques of observation like controlled vs uncontrolled and structured vs unstructured etc.

The ninth chapter is about the questionnaire, as a tool of data collection. It also tells about the standards, recommendations and norms for formulation of a questionnaire. Many examples of questionnaire are also given to make understand about the questionnaire in a better way. The tenth chapter is about experimental research design. It gives a practical knowledge about the lab and field experiments. Here the cause and effect relationship is also explained to clarify about validity and reliability. The eleventh chapter is about the measurement of variable or set of items which should be included into a particular research. Here customs, traditions, culture and demographic variables are explained. The twelfth chapter is about the measurement scaling. It contains nominal, ordinal, interval and ratio. Here reliability and validity concept is also discussed with practical example which tells about the authenticity of the research. How the result of the research can be analyzed in the research, is also discussed in this chapter.

The thirteen chapter is about the sampling, sampling design decision and sampling size. Here sampling is broadly classified into probabilistic sampling and non probabilistic sampling. Sample size is determined by level of precision and confidence designed in research.

As we know proper sampling is must for population parameter and hypothesis testing. The fourteen chapter is about quntative data analysis. In this chapter the initial steps for procedure for analyzing data s given once. Here the editing, coding and categorizing are also discussed with very beautiful example is given as Excelsior Enterprises case, finally the goodness of data is also discussed with Cronbach's Alpha. The fifteen chapter is about quantitative data analysis & hypothesis testing it also contain type-I and type-II errors with statistical power. Different type of dummy variable, multicolinearity and moderate regression analysis are also discussed with SPSS software. The most interesting thing here is the resent analysis is also tangent with interesting example by SPSS. The sixteenth chapter is about the qualitative data analysis. It helps a lot in formulation of inferences and theory formulation. Miles and Humberman (1999) approach are also discussed. The special thing in the form of process as data analysis, data reduced, data rearranged, integrated to form theory through coding and categorizing is also given. The last and seventeenth chapter is about the formulation of research report. It contains the objectives, purposes, composition of the intended audience etc. in simple words, it tells the complete process of writing research repeat and it also tells about the examples of different thesis sot that the research and presentation of research can be more effective and better.

This book defines that research is an integral part of life; it brings continuously improvement and help in growing progressively. The skill-building approach provides a practical perspective on how research can be applied in real business situations. In nut shell it can be said, this book helps a lot to clear the concepts of research, research process and other factors effecting on research.

During comparison a lot of difference found between $5^{th}$ and $6^{th}$ edition. The Sixth edition includes a range of new material on alternative approaches to business research, including three new chapters on: The Critical Literature Review, Observation, and Questionnaires. Other chapters on The Broad Problem Area and Defining the Problem Statement, Research Design, Interviews and The Research Report have also been substantially revised. Examples are drawn from different areas of business - such as human resources management, strategic management, operations management, finance, accounting, and information management - to provide students with a comprehensive overview of the applications of research methods.

This book is very knowledgeable, interesting and better for those who want to study business research into a deep manner. After reading this book I recommend it to engineering students for making them perfect engineer.

# 3D PRINTING BUILDINGS: AN ADVANCE LEARNING FOR MAKING OF AN EXPERT CIVIL ENGINEER

Author: Gourav,

Lecturer,

Department of Civil Engineering,

Jind Polytechnic College, Jind (126102) Haryana.

## 1. INTRODUCTION

3D printing, or additive producing is that the construction of a three-dimensional article or object from a CAD model or a digital 3D model. The term "3D printing" will visit a range of action or procedure during which material is deposited, joined or coagulated beneath pc management to make a three-dimensional object, with material being side along (including plastics, liquids or powder form grains being consolidated together), generally layer after layer.

As of 2021, the preciseness, repeatability and material vary of 3D printing have exaggerated to the purpose that some 3D printing processes area unit thought-about viable as an industrial-production technology, in accordance with which the term additive producing are often used synonymously with 3D printing. One among the key benefits of 3D printing is that the ability to supply terribly complicated shapes or geometries that may be otherwise not possible to construct by hand, as well as hollow components or components with internal truss structures to scale back weight. Fused deposit model (FDM), that uses a continual filament of a thermoplastic polymer like material, is that the most common 3D printing in use as of 2021.

3D printing models are often designed with a package (CAD), a photogrammetric software system, and a 3D scanner or an easy photographic camera. 3D prototypes for print designed with CAD result in a smaller range of errors in reference to different ways. Inaccuracies in 3D written prototypes are often discovered and stuck before printing starts. The action or the procedure of geometric knowledge preparation for 3D tricks exploitation manual modelling resembles bound sorts of plastic arts, as an example sculpting. The procedure of 3D scanning is gathering digital knowledge relating to kind and look of an entity and coming up with a pc model created on the idea of that knowledge.

Prototypes are often saved as a file and an easy USB flash drive will function memory cloud for every project. The example is often altered before printing yet as throughout the method.

Normally, 3D printing has targeting polymers or other fine material for writing by explanation for compound materials manufacturing and process ease notwithstanding, this system has quick developed not just for the assembly of various polymers, however additionally for concrete and ceramics that makes 3D printing a universal production alternative.

The Author's plan is to offer or provide a quick concept however this technology are often used for construct a building and the way this technology becomes is in trend in construction field and may solve several downside in construction as exploitation this we are able to give any form or shape to our building with nearly zero waste turn out throughout construction with less labour enclosed.

## 2. CONSTRUCTION 3D PRINTING BUILDING

This chapter describes concrete 3D printing building. The demonstration of construction printing on the location was the conception of the chapter. The main purpose of read for this chapter is to indicate the practicality, gift prospects and challenges and its future outlook of the development 3D printing technology use for construct a building and plenty of different engineering science comes.

### 2.1 What is Construction 3D Printing?

A construction 3D printer could be a device or machine capable of printing constructions layer after layer. Concrete 3D printing resembles methodology employed by consolidated deposition modelling machines producing is as follows: colourless substance is ironed through the nozzle in layers to come up with structures in 3D.

**Figure -1 (Construction 3D robotic arm printer)**

The advantages or the benefits of concrete 3D printing within the building business area unit time saving and effective use of resources in distinction to traditional building practices. However, it's important to state that 3D printers aren't ready to turn or replace out utterly useful buildings at this point.

In home 3D printing, frames and walls area unit created and, after that, electricity, tube or windows settlement need instalment severally. Structures as platforms, seats or exterior decorations could also be created with concrete 3D printers yet.

The extrusion technique is applied by 3D printers. Explicit 3D printers contain a spinning mechanical arm whereas different area unit analogous to ultra-large desktop FDM (gantry-style) ones.

Paste like components, as an example concrete, area unit applied as filament in every case. In easy terms, this method resembles the unfold of cake coating with a pastry bag. Thus, the substance is squeezed out of a special nozzle making layers.

The printer layer by layer generates base and walls of a building on the bottom that is a piece surface. However, brick molds area unit factory-made with bound concrete 3D printers. After that, the bricks area unit placed on high of every different by hand or with a robotic arm.

## 2.2 Fundamental operating Principles of 3d Printing

Irrespective of the business application or style of 3D printer in use, the operational mechanism is that the same the essential stages of this method from the model to the ultimate written object area unit explained below:

### Preparation of 3D Model

The first step is that the production of a 3D model created employing a 3D CAD program. There are a unit variety of software system on the market to suit several style functions, many of them area unit wide used at intervals the 3D printing house including; Autodesk, Fusion 360, Solid Works, Rhinoceros, Google Sketch up, etc.

3D scanning is another methodology accustomed scan real or physical objects, that area unit born-again into CAD virtual models which will be written in 3D.

### The STL FILE

In the second step, the finished CAD model is exported to .STL file format. This file extension stands for Stereolithography, or typically normal Tessellation Language, a basic a part of the 3D writing. As mentioned within the introduction, this method was unreal by Charles Hull. The STL file records the info of 3D models. This format interprets solely the surface pure mathematics of a 3D object without any illustration of colour, texture or different attributes of the model.

### The Slicing Program

In the third step, the STL file is loaded into a slicing program additionally spoken because the slicer. There are a unit variety of slicing software system on the market, some area unit proprietary; i.e.

the slicer forms a part of the 3D printer's interface and is customised to a particular whole of 3D printers, others area unit open supply and may be used across totally different platforms interface and is customised to a particular whole of 3D printers, others area unit open supply and may be used across totally different platforms.

### The Slicing Operation

The fourth step is that the actual slicing operation. The slicing program creates directions referred to as the geode in order that the printer is aware of a way to create the model. Here the STL model is sliced into many layers; every purpose on each layer having its distinctive mathematician coordinates. All the coordinates' area unit born-again into a collection of directions referred to as the G-code that is that the language understood by the 3D printer.

### The Printing operation

The final step is that the printing stage wherever the info of the already sliced model (G-code) is distributed to the printer. Once the printer receives the command to print, the print head begins its motion on totally different axes as determined by the G-code. The model is being designed layer upon layer.

### Working & Finishing

This is a bonus step needed in cases wherever there's material residue created as support for the model. This residue doesn't kind a part of the particular model however is critical for its build. The residue has to be fastidiously scraped, plucked, agitated or blown out counting on the character of the fabric. It ought to be through with care therefore as to not injury the model.

After this, it's no obligatory to treat the surface of the model by smoothing or filing, coating and different finishing techniques to convey it the required look. Fig 2. Is an illustration of the diagram of the 3D writing?

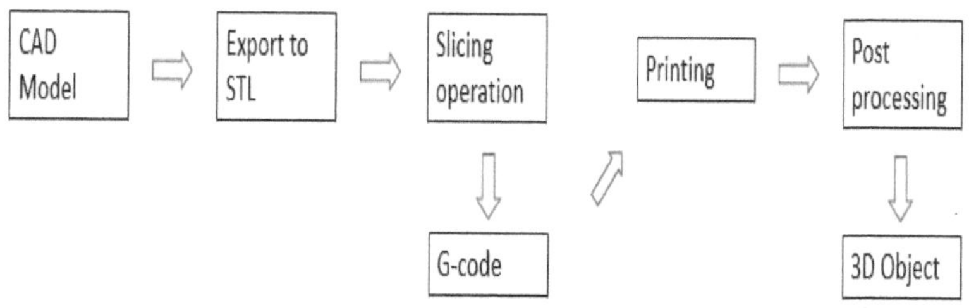


**Fig-2 (Flow diagram)**

## 2.3 CLASSIFICATION OF 3D PRINTED BUILDING SUPPORTED TOTALLY DIFFERENT METHODOLOGY

### 2.3.1 Contour crafting (CC) Technique

Contour crafting could be a methodology of stratified producing method that uses chemical compound, ceramic suspension, cement, and a range of different materials and mixes to make giant scale objects with swish surface end. It absolutely was 1st undraped in 1996 at the University of Southern CA (USC); the oldest technique that has been developed thus far and continues to be being developed beneath its discoverer, Dr. Berokh Khoshnevis at the USC and CC business firm.

It replaces standard 'cast-in-place' ways with a layer-by-layer approach. This new manner of thinking offers automation a far higher probability to penetrate and reach the construction field .It gets obviate the necessity for ancient formwork.

The contour crafting technique adopts the principle of the consolidated Deposition Modelling or fused deposition modeling technique that involves extruding cement primarily based paste against a trowel that enables a swish surface end created through the build-up of later layers. Today, cement primarily based paste is that the alternative material for CC. The extrusion Nozzle, of that there are a minimum of four separate, styles. The CC machine is gantry primarily based for a 3-axis management of its specialised nozzles.

This technique are often applied for varied kinds of construction as well as buildings, as well as infrastructure that might embody foundations, slabs, walls, pylons, etc. there's additionally extra-terrestrial construction, that is, building on the Moon and Mars or any other planet of our universe for planetary exploration, exploitation, habitation and establishment. Contour crafting corporation has collaborated with NASA and different house organisations during this field of use of its technology and has excelled to receive high recognition not solely within the America, however varied space programs in varied countries.

### 2.3.2 Concrete Printing Technique

This technology is commonly said as 3D Concrete printing (3DCP). Developed at Loughborough University Britain since 2004; a collaboration between Dr. Prince Rupert Soar and Dr. Richard Boswell. The assembly of the primary concrete machine happened in 2006. 3DCP is comparable in essence to the contour crafting but, its nozzle is intended to own the capability to vary its resolution, permitting the deposition of each bulk materials and fine detail at intervals identical method. Nozzle size will be adjusted for selective deposition of fine or coarse concrete pastes counting on the amount of detail desired. Nozzle management for concrete printing may be framing primarily based, robotic arm or by delta system. The robotic arm permits multi-axis nozzle management to facilitate what's said as freeform construction. This system has been wide adopted and changed to be used by numerous groups worldwide.

### 2.3.33 D-Shape Technique

Developed in 2008, the D-Shape 3D printing technique could be a Layer by layer writing that by selection prints liquid onto a bed of sand and binder combine. The liquid creates a reaction with the sand combine and transforms it into a stone like material. The technique is known as once a personal Italian company supported by Dini. this system is distinct at intervals the trade as a result of not like the CC and concrete printing that area unit Extrusion primarily based following the FDM principle, the D-Shape employs the Binder running principle on an outsized scale for sand primarily based materials.

The liquid creates a reaction with the catalyst within the sand mixture and therefore the written sand transforms into a solid sand-stone-like material. This system is really free morpheme because it needs no support material since the item is made on a bed of sand. The sand bed is the support for the item this ensures even additional style freedom as all types of complicated or knotty shapes will be accomplished. This system but needs in depth post process to get rid of the written object out of the combination pile, there's conjointly got to treat the surfaces by sanding, polishing, spraying or painting counting on the specified end.

## 2.4 Main Components of A Typical 3D machine

The main components put in in 3D printing thermoplastics material and concrete are the coordinate controls and thus the extruder than unharnessed the material. The organization machinery are typically comprised of assorted components therefore on achieve the desired coordinates. For example, a frame crane mechanism is typically used, or a robotic arm can reach to the locations where the 3D print extrudes materials. The frame system and thus the robotic arm use rotary motors to make linear and motion movement. The machine system moves the tip effectors or extruder to the desired coordinate to be ready to 3D print concrete. The tip effectors are that the situation on the printer that is associated with the coordinate purpose on the laptop assisted vogue model. The processed manufacturing of the model moves the tip nozzle to the specific coordinate points to 3D print objects by creating a nozzle path that 3D prints objects layer by layer. The laptop model is sliced into varied layers and thus the nozzle stacked concrete on high of the previously sliced layer. To stack concrete, the concrete mixture ought to do not have any slump and high early strength once exploit the nozzle.

Associate in nursing example of the 3D concrete printer operative is shown in Figure 3. As a relatively stiff continuous filament.

**FIG.- 3 (3D MACHINE)**

In figure 3, a frame system uses rotary motors to form linear zed movements inside the three-dimensional axis space. Each of its motors is to blame for a coordinate frame; therefore, there are three motors and axes. A robotic arm that threeD prints in addition uses three rotary motors to realize 3 degrees of freedom to 3D print. The organization is based on cylindrical coordinates rather than thinker coordinates. Robotic arms with quite three degrees of freedom are typically used to 3D print objects. the use of a robotic arm that has quite three degrees of freedom is used to develop radio carpal joint motion to 3D print at angles in exhausting to achieve areas in acceleration of 1.8 m/s in x,y, and z coordinate. The components of a 3D machine are shown in Figure given below.

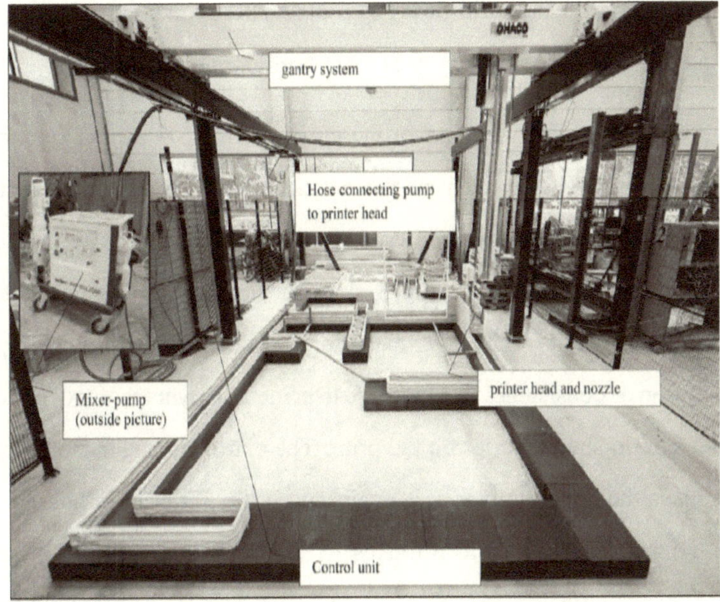


Fig 2 : 3DCP facility at the TU Eindhoven, with some examples of printed objects

## Different component of 3D Printing Machine

The extruder mechanism will activate to induce down material once the machine has reached the coordinate where the extruder must be compelled to dispense material. A rotating motor is also included in the extruder, which rotates whenever the coordinate mechanism is set to a desired coordinate for printing. A thermoplastic printer's extruder differs significantly from a concrete 3D printer's. A spool and a rotating motor make up a thermoplastic printer. The filament is attached to the motor, which moves it through a heated nozzle. The heated nozzle turns the solid thermoplastic into a liquid, which is subsequently dispersed onto the 3D print and solidifies. The concrete 3D printer extruder works by putting a grout pump on top of a 3D printing platform.

To appropriately lay down the concrete, the 3D printer's nozzle is usually changed by altering the nozzle orientation. To ensure that the extrusion is properly ordered down, the nozzle should be rotated in a clockwise orientation. Fig 3 shows a nozzle for fine constancy printing that uses layer by layer extrusion. Because of the printing's high resolution or consistency, it's possible to print thin layers that are refined to have a finished exterior on the print. The extrusion auger motor that produces the concrete before it is placed on the 3D print is housed in this nozzle. The printer then moves within the printer's direction and orientation to precisely 3D print the problem. As a result, there are two extrusion systems.

### 3. Materials

The fundamental components for 3D printing of items are fine-grained mixes that differ from typical concrete with a low slump value. Every company creates its own substances, which relate to the printer and its nozzle composition, as well as certain features of the produced product. The primary concrete properties for a 3D printer are durability, rate of hardening and setting, and property. The grade of cement, fillers, and plasticizers, as well as the combination structure, influence concrete selections.

Users can offer components of varying quality, height, and dimension, ranging from modest bailiwick constructions such as garden beds and seats to full residences, platforms, and tower construction, using already produced combinations.

## 4. Merits of Construction 3D Printing

C3DP has been same to hold voluminous promise as a result of it utilizes the power of computing and AI to form tailored homes among a short quantity. This development may well be most useful for low-income housing.

Some of the Key deserves of 3D printing of buildings include:

- Faster rate of construction

- Reduced construction waste / environmental friendliness

- Cost savings in some prospective

- Safety

- Design freedom

- Construction Accuracy

1. Speed of Construction

Concrete printers have the capability to print giant volume of walls among a brief timeframe. There are reports that tiny homes are written among twenty four hours. This is often one in all the options that create this technology engaging. It ought to be noted but that the printing speed applies solely to the walls and in some cases formwork building; this implies that the time is shortened for the erection of the walls and formwork alone, the time it takes for different jobs like finishes and different installations stay an equivalent.

## 2. Reduced Construction Waste / Environmental Friendliness

A study administered enumerates 3 major factors contributory to construction material waste generated on building sites including-

1. Make over contrary to drawing and specification

2. Style changes or revisions

3. Waste from uneconomical shapes

3. Price savings

Labour prices are driven down by 3D printing; it takes 3-4 folks to create with a 3D printer as against a lot of hands needed in standard building.

4. Safety

Building with a 3D printer is safe. Globally, construction staff is thrice a lot of possible to be killed and doubly as possible to be out of action as staff in different occupations. Within the U.S.A., it absolutely was reportable that the development sector accounts for two hundredth of labour connected fatalities and twelve-tone system of disabling injuries. the protection advantages offered by 3D printing is especially required in African country wherever unsafe Building practices persist unrestrained, 3D printing impacts absolutely during this regard, but in cases of offsite fabrication, there may well be associated risks.

The COVID nineteen pandemic has additionally recently unconcealed the vast safety impact of this technology. The requirement for style shifts has become imperative because they apply of social distancing and new job procedures are often accommodated with 3D printing. Whereas it takes 3-4 folks to figure aboard the 3D printer, safety protocols are often adhered to and construction will persist unaffected by pandemics.

5. Style freedom

Many shapes and {architectural fine arts beaux arts} forms that are troublesome and dear to understand with standard construction don't seem to be a limitation for 3D printing. The 3D printer creates special shapes with ease, The Architects' dream to push building style boundaries are often completed at no additional price. This presents opportunities for personalization and therefore the chance of deviating from example building while not extra price implications. In India and in entire world, this may facilitate to push the Architects' creative thinking on the far side construction boundaries.

6. Accuracy and exactness

Construction errors are virtually not possible to avoid once building conventionally, 3D printers will manufacture buildings at tier of accuracy a dead ringer for the CAD model it's created from, and therefore the quality of a building is greatly wedged by this.

## 5. Constraints and Drawback of 3d Printing for Buildings

Despite its tremendous deserves, there are still limitations to the present technology. A couple of of them are examined here

1. Lack of Codes and Standards

Given that the technology remains in its early stages, there are however to be any standards and codes guiding its use. Currently, ASTM committee F42 and ISO/TC 261members are engaged on developing a customary for AM. However, there's no committee and customary for C3DP Lack of standards makes building approvals troublesome to get for 3D written buildings in most countries

2. Not suited to high rise construction

There are major setbacks thanks to the shortcoming to create vertically with 3D printing isn't however attainable, it's troublesome to travel on the far side 2 floors. It's been recognized that cities wherever housing is most in demand are already densely inhabited and densely designed. Till 3D printing will build taller, it's going to not be as useful for mass housing as anticipated because the technology advances, these constraints are going to be checked. Currently a proposal for crane based mostly 3D printing of a high rise building in Dubai is in review.

## 6. FUTURE OUTLOOK

### 3D PRINT ON MARS

3D printing on Mars allows for construction to begin before people arrive on the Red Planet. 3D printing robots are poised to create a habitable environment for astronauts, reducing the need for human building once the world becomes unsuitable. The atmosphere of Mars is composed of 96% carbonic acid gas and is 100 times diluting than that of Earth.

The average temperature is -81 degrees Fahrenheit. With temperatures ranging from -284 to 86 degrees Fahrenheit, Gabriel Daniel Fahrenheit is a physicist. The artificial environment may be required to safeguard astronauts from radiation and sustain Earth-like atmospheric conditions. The internal structure of a 3D printed structure can be regulated and sealed from the Martian environment. Because 3D printing builds monolithic structures, the structure can be sealed.

### 3D written environs

The living setting on Mars would force a large number of building materials and construction solutions to be ready to produce a lovable civilization. National Aeronautics and Space Administration hosted a centennial challenge to encourage housing solutions for the primary structures on Mars. The competition is termed the 3D written environs Challenge. Many voters' inventors groups have joined the competition to 3D print a functioning sheltering. The goal is to form a shelter that may house four astronauts for a year with concerns to the mechanical, electrical, and plumbing systems. The shelter additionally takes into consideration practicality for spacesuits and rovers on Mars. The challenge aims to advance construction technology in respect to housing and shelter on Earth whereas developing technology for a Mars environs.

## Zopherus

This group has given specific consideration to the development approach on Mars, where 3D printing could be disrupted by winds and temperature variations. The team's solution is to create a spacecraft that can house and protect the 3D printer while it constructs the shelter. The spacecraft would then elevate itself on top of the 3D written house, erecting a shelter in the process. In addition, the spaceship serves as an emergency pressure vessel. The spacecraft's shelter is made up of two layers: an HDPE layer and a layer of Mars concrete. The shelter's numerous layers protect it from temperature variations and radiation. The community will grow because the housing structure is modular.

## CONCRETE REGOLITH combine style

Building a civil infrastructure on Mars could be possible because to advances in 3D printing technology. Building on Mars is also economically feasible because it has a regolith roof that may be used for undisturbed construction. 3D printing is a rapidly growing field in construction that creates concrete formwork layer by layer without the use of moulds or forms. Because the feedstock used in 3D printing concrete must have a body Associate in Nursingd workability that can flow via an extrusion and dynamic pump system, it must be a combination style that combines fine particles. The advantages of concrete include 3D printable supported buildable layers, system flow ability, and minimal gravitative out gassing.

**3D PRINTED BUILDING IN INDIA**

Indian government decide to faceplate house to each family till the end of 2022 under the skim "HOUSING FOR ALL" and by using this construction technology we can built it faster rate so govt. can achieve their target.

In India a student of IIT Madras has built a 3D printed building at a very low cost. This is built up In 600 square feet, single storey only in five days.

In India, Larsen and turbo (L&T) company has also created a building by using this technology. The building, which has a modest floor area of 65 $m^2$, was built utilising a large-format concrete 3D printer provided by OEM COBOD and is made of a locally produced 3D printable concrete mix designed by L&T's own in-house team. The building, which is located near the city of Chennai at the company's Kanchipuram site, even features integrated reinforcement bars and is fully compliant with all of India's construction codes.

## THE ROLE OF STATISTICS IN QUALITY ENGINEERING.

Author: Dr. Gaurav,
Assistant Professor,
Department of Management Studies,
Jind Institute of Engineering and Technology, Jind (126102) Haryana.

### ABSTRACT

The role of statistics in quality engineering plays a vital role. Statistics is part and partial for engineering as it enhance the quality of human the demand, production and profit. It gives better way of doing work and create constructive environment. This chapter includes the importance of statistics for engineering, the tests used for engineering to enhance the production and to enhance the level of thinking of an engineer. It also contains the statistical quality control measures for engineering.

### INTRODUCTION

In previous time statistics was used to collect the information related to crime, population, wealth, force etc. for construction of monetary policy, fiscal policy and certain human activities. Different people take different meaning from statistics. For engineer it is demand, profit, inflation and deflation. But this word has a deep sense and it is associated to all the activities of human being.

- For cricket fan, it is the number of fans and followers.

- For power production sector it is the unit of power generated.

- For medical it is the number of patient.

- For bank and financial institution, it is the currency, share, debenture etc.

Therefore, Statistics is the study of the collection, analysis, interpretation and organization of data. It deals with all aspects of data including the planning of data collection in terms of the design of surveys and experiments.

**Methods of statistical data collection**

Data can be collected by census method by including each and every element of survey; and sampling is a technique which include few elements which show all the characteristics of population.

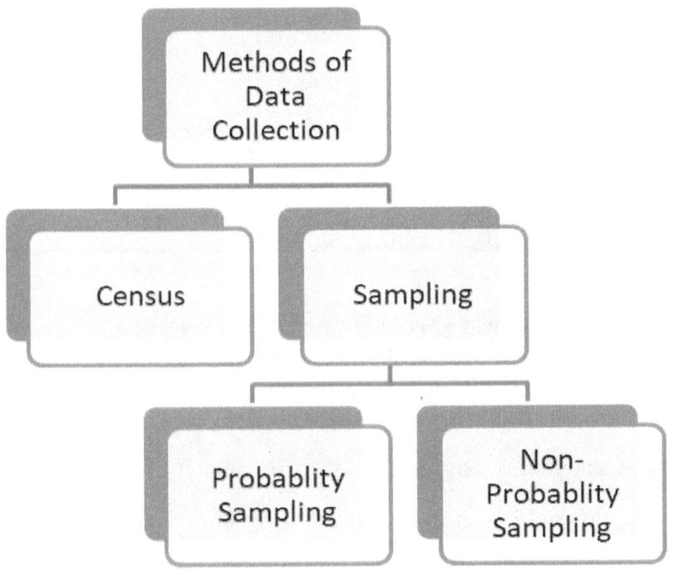


**Figure-1 (Methods of Data Collection)**

## PRESENTATION OF DATA

Data can be shown or represented in various form by using table and chart i.e pie chart, mean chart, range chart, bar chart, web chart and much more. On the basis of the use that can be presented. Frequency chart, pie chart and histogram has been shown here to understand it in better way. The example is as follows:

## FREQUENCY TABLE

Frequency table show the number of variable used with percentage and commutative percentage so that it can be easy to understand.

**Gender**

| | | Frequency | Percent | Valid Percent | Cumulative Percent |
|---|---|---|---|---|---|
| Valid | Male | 331 | 49.5 | 49.5 | 49.5 |
| | Female | 306 | 45.7 | 45.7 | 95.2 |
| | Transgender | 32 | 4.8 | 4.8 | 100.0 |
| | Total | 669 | 100.0 | 100.0 | |

**Table-1 (Frequency Table of Gender)**

## BAR CHART

The mentioned bar chart shows the annual income of different category of people. It show the data in more understandable way.

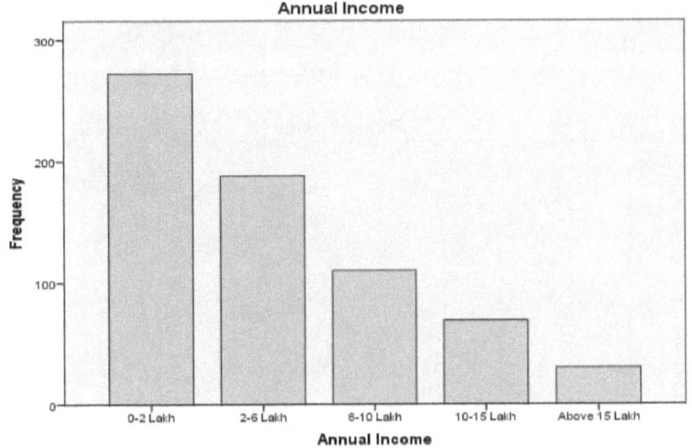


**Figure-2 (Bar Chart of Annual Income)**

## PIE CHART

Pie chart helps to understand and present the date into well and more understandable way. It show the data in percentage or angles i.e 360. The mention pie chart shows the data in term of gender as Male, Female and Transgender.

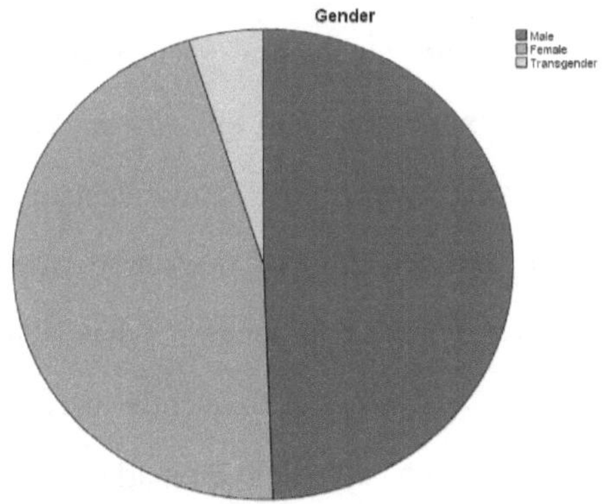


**Figure-3 (Gender Classification)**

**HISTOGRAM-** Histogram shows the data in bar form of data representation.

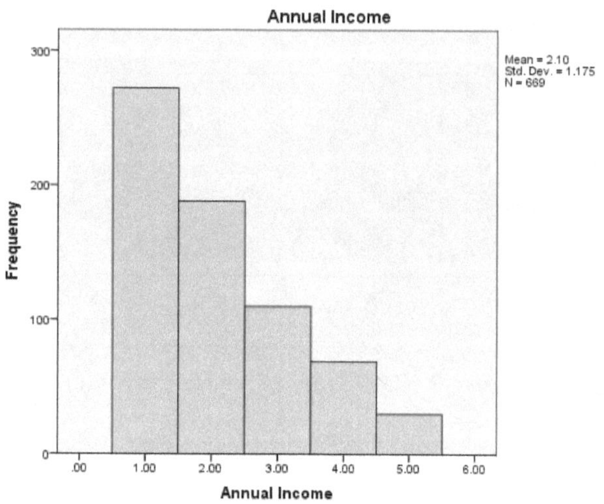


**Figure-4 (Histogram of Annual Income)**

## USE OF STATISTICS FOR GENERATING MARKETING INFORMATION

Statistical techniques are an integral part of modern marketing research, which in turn provides the input to many marketing decisions of both profit and nonprofit organizations. These decisions include the generation, evaluation, and selection of marketing strategies. Stock market analysts also use statistics to forecast what is happening in the economy. Statistical analysis are frequently used in providing information for making decision in the field for marketing it is necessary first to find out what can be sold and to evolve suitable strategy. A skill full analysis of data on production purchasing power, man power, habits of competitors, habits of consumer, transportation cost should be consider to take any attempt to establish a new market. Statistics can help the marketer to achieve both of those goals as well as evaluate the success of the marketing effort and provide data on which to base changes to the market program. Statistics are applied in marketing in many ways, such as:

- To know about marketing trends

- To evaluate the goodwill and potential customers.

- To strengthen the communication activities.

- To know about the customers satisfaction.

- To know about the make or buy decision.

- To know about the basic need of society.

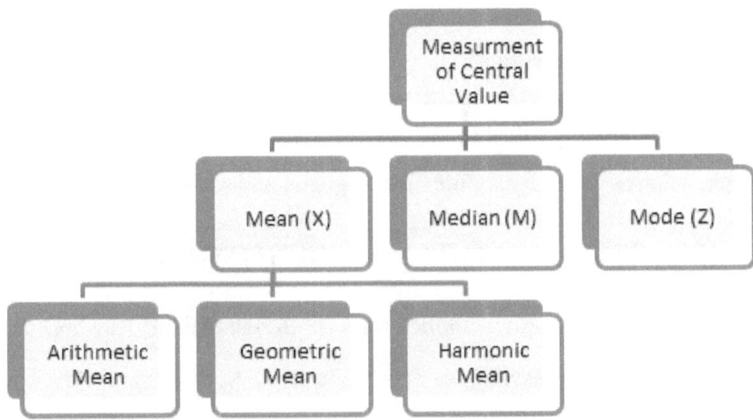


**Figure-5 (Measurement of Central Tendency in Marketing Information)**

## USE OF STATISTICS IN PRODUCTION SECTOR

In the field of production, statistical data play a very important role. The decision about what to produce? How to produce? When to produce? For whom to produce? Is based largely on statistical analysis. The manufacturing industry produces goods from raw materials or assembles products from components. It supplies the domestic and international markets and some specialist niche market. The powerful technique of control charts and inspection plans are very important aspect of statistical theory used in manufacturing industries. Statistics are applied in production as follows

- To assist in designing, building, improving and ensuring the reliability of a wide variety of manufactured products such as appliances, plastic materials, aircraft engines and locomotives.

- To control the quality of the manufactured products so that it conforms to specifications.

- To provide information to economic indicators about sales, stock, salaries and wages, purchase of goods and services.

## USE OF STATISTICS FOR ACCOUNTING INFORMATION

The ever increasing applications of the statistical data and the advanced statistical techniques in the Chartered Accounts and Cost and Works Accountants examinations curriculum. Statistics has innumerable applications in accountancy and auditing.

- For evaluation of the assets of the business concerns.

- Statistical data on some macro variables like income, expenditure, investment, profits, production, savings, etc.,

- Revaluating the accounting records based on historical costs of assets after adjusting for the changes in the purchasing power of money. » Used in forecasting profits, determination of trends, computation of financial ratios.

**USES OF DISPERSION IN STATISTICS-** using of dispersion is essential part in the production sector.

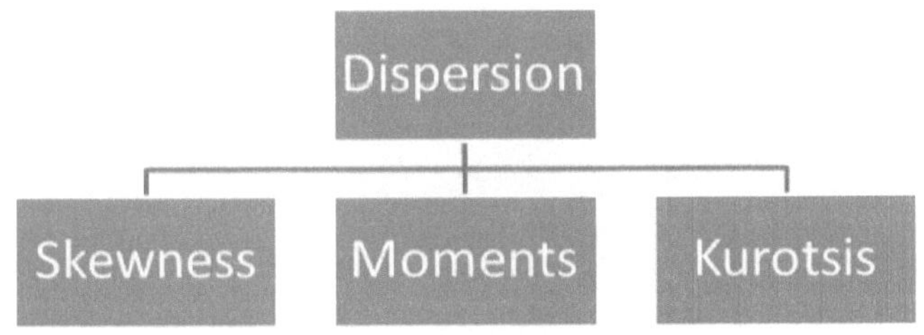


**Figure-6 (Classification of Dispersion)**

**Use Of Statistics In Human Resources Management**

Statistical data used in personnel administration relating to wages, cost of living, incentive plans, effect of labor dispute/ unrest on the production, performance standards, etc,.the demand and supply of staffs is always fluctuating in business, therefore statistics helps the HR team.

- In Recruiting and training of staff.

- To identify areas of weakness where improvement is needed.

- To identify compensation programs such as pension schemes.

                    The Making of an Expert Engineer

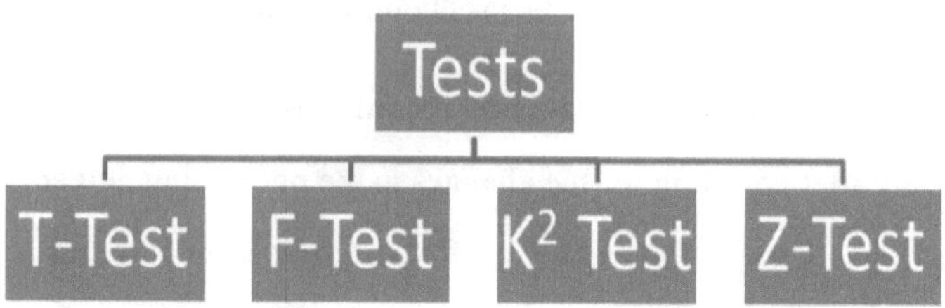


**Figure-7 (Tests for Human Resource Management)**

# REQUIREMENTS OF DESIGN OF CONCRETE STRUCTURE FOR APERFECT CIVIL ENGINEER.

Author: Sinhmar Gurbaksh Singh,
Lecturer,
Department of Civil Engineering,
Jind Polytechnic College, Jind (126102) Haryana.

## INTRODUCTION

In Civil Engineering for construction of structure Concrete is most widely used material. It consists of cement act as binding material, water and inert material called aggregate and sometimes Admixture is also used . Hardening of concrete is caused due to chemical reaction between Cement and water called Hydration process ,which take place continue for long time .

Due to this hydration process Concrete become stronger .

Concrete is very strong in compression but it's tensile strength is very low. It's tensile strength is about 10 -15% of its compressive strength.

### Reinforced cement concrete

- The steel bars in structures are used mainly in tension side , because in Tension side Tensile Strength of concrete is low and external tensile load is resisted by steel only . The steel bars are also used in compression side when the external load on structure is more heavy.

- We can say that Steel bars in concrete is soul of structure because without steel concrete is nothing. Steel bars provide Strength in concrete and in the form of Distribution bars it resist the temperature and shrinkage crack in structure.

### Uses of Reinforced Concrete

- Buildings( Foundation ,beam, column, slab)

- Flyovers and under passes

- Construction in sea like harbour

- Stair cases

- Road and Rail Bridges

- Chimneys and Towers

- Retaining Walls and RCC water tank

### Advantages Reinforced cement concrete

- **Strength:** The RCC provide good strength in compression as well as in tension.

- **Economy:** It is cheaper than Steel and  prestressed  concrete . Therefore overall economy using by RCC is very low.

- **Durability:** R.C.C. structures are durable . The term durability express resistance to corrosion of steel , chemical attack and weather.

- **Ductility:** The steel reinforcement provide ductility to the R.C.C. structure. Therefore Structure give warning before failure

- **Material Availability:** The raw materials which are used in R.C.C. like cement, sand, aggregate, water and steel are easily available

- **Fire Resistance:** RCC structures are more fire resistant than other materials like wood and steel.

**Requirements of Concrete**

A good concrete should have following requirement.

(i) The concrete should me mixed properly without segregation and bleeding . Segregation is process in which all the aggregate in concrete are separate and settled down . Bleeding is a process in which water from concrete is rise at upper surface (i.e. water separate from cement paste)

(ii) Concrete should be compacted properly by removing air void from it. Due to this Density of concrete becomes maximum.

(iii) Curing of concrete is required for complete hydration process of cement. It provide sufficient Strength to the concrete. Minimum 7 days Curing is required for concrete.

(iv) The water cement ratio should be considered in proper way . It should not be less than 0.45 , if below this value then honeycomb structure is formed.

(v) The concrete mix should be designed properly and all the necessary ingredients are in right proportions.

(vi) The water used for mixing should be free from all harmful substances. Water should be such that as we use in drinking purpose.

(vii) The fine and coarse aggregate in concrete should be hard, strong and durable. For most R.C.C. works, 20 mm size of aggregate commonly used.

(Viii) The cement used for R.C.C. work should be of good quality and should free from Lumps and Humidity. Cement should not be more old, as the cement old Strength be decreased.( 3 month old cement 20% , 6 month old cement 30% , 1 year old 40%, and 2 year old cement 50% strength Decrease)

**Grade of Concrete:**

- Concrete grades are expressed by letter M followed by a number.

The letter 'M' represent the mix and the number represents the characteristic compressive strength of concrete in N/mm2.

- The characteristic strength of concrete is determined for 150 mm size cube at 28 days.

- **"The characteristic compressive strength of concrete is defined as that strength of concrete below which not more than 5 percent of the test results are expected to fall".**

- **The various grades of concrete as per their use are listed below:**

1. For R.C.C. work - not less than M20.

2. For post-tensioning works – not lower than M35

3. For pre-tensioned concrete – not lower than M40

4. For R.C.C work in Sea water – not less than M30

5. For plain cement concrete work in Sea water – not less than M 20

6. For Water tank construction- minimum M30

**Grade of Steel Reinforcement**

- Steel grades are expressed by letter Fe followed by a number.

- The letter 'Fe' refers to the Ferrous and the number represents the characteristic strength of steel or yield strength of steel in N/mm2 (The characteristic Strength of steel is taken to be it'syield strength).

- Commonly Fe250 , Fe415 and Fe500 grade of steel, TMT ( Thermo- Mechanically Treated )bars are used in Construction .

- The mild steel i.e. Fe250 bars are very ductile it give warning before failure due to this property but it's tensile strength is very low as compared to HYSD bars .So in Civil Engineering structures HYSD bars are more preferred.

- Fe415 and Fe500 are called HYSD bars ( high yield strength deformed bars)

- The yield strength of Fe 415 and Fe500 is taken at the proof strain of 0.2% which is called 0.2% proof stress( because in case of

HYSD there is no proper yield point on stress strain curve).

- The modulus of elasticity of all steels taken  as equal to 2 x 105N/mm2.

- Mild steel mainly used in lateral ties and light structures.

The stress-strain curve for mild steel and HYSD steel is given in Fig.  It shows a clear, definite yield point.

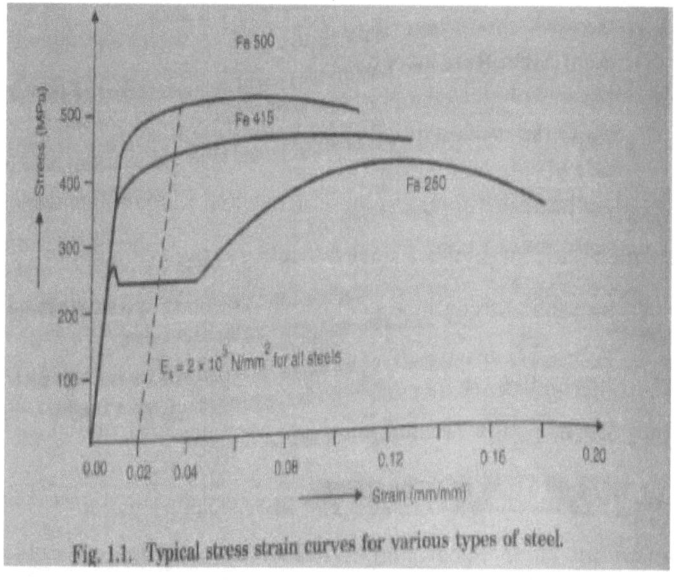


Fig. 1.1. Typical stress strain curves for various types of steel.

## Method of RCC design

Various methods used for the design of R.C.C. structures are as follows:

(i) Working stress method.

(ii) Ultimate load method.

(iii)Limit state method

## Limit State Method

- Now a days Limit state method is Used . This is the most reliable method which takes into account the ultimate strength of the structure and also the serviceability requirements.

- The limit state can be achieved due to mainly either:

(i)  Limit state of collapse ( Flexure, compression, Shear, Torsion is considered) Limit state of serviceability( Deflection, cracking, vibration , corrosion is considered)

## What is Limit State?

The acceptable limit for safety and serviceability of structure or member just before failure is termed as Limit State.

The structure become unfit for use if it reaches at limit state.

- **Safety:** Safety is criteria which ensures that structure should be safe against collapse of structure not only under working load but also under overload.

- **Serviceability:** Serviceability is the criteria which ensure the  performance of structure under working loads without discomfort to user due to excessive deflections, cracking, vibration etc.

**What is Partial safety factor?**

•The factor by which characteristics value of material are reduced or increased  termed as partial safety factor

**Characteristic Strength of material :**

The "characteristic Strength of a material" is the value of strength below which not more than 5 percent of test results  are expected to fall.

The characteristic Strength of concrete is determined from the compressive strength of 150mm concrete cubes as per Indian standard.

The characteristic strength of steel  is the yield strength in tension for hot rolled bars or mild steel and 0.2 percent proof stress / yield strength for cold worked or HYSD bars

**Characteristic load** :Characteristic load is that value of load which has 95% probability of not being exceeded during the life of structure.

**Design load:**

It is the load for which structure is to be designed. The design load is obtained by multiplying the partial factor of safety with characteristic load.

**Note: During designing of structure, for increasing the safety and serviceability of structure we are required reduced value of Characteristic strength of materials and increased value of Characteristic load.**

**Partial safety factors for materials:**

The factors by which characteristic Strength value of material are reduced is known as partial safety factor. **As per IS: 456 code ,the** partial safety factor for concrete is 1.5 and for steel it is 1.15.

The factor of safety of concrete is more as compared to steel is because in concrete  chance of variation in strength due to **improper compaction, inadequate curing and variation in the proportion of ingredient. But steel is manufactured in factories where great care is to be take place.**

**Design strength = ( characteristic Strength) / partial safety factor**

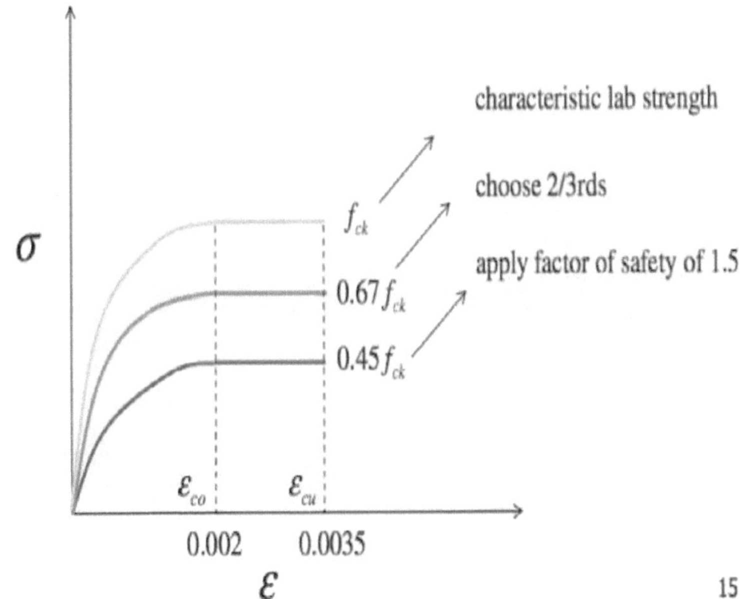

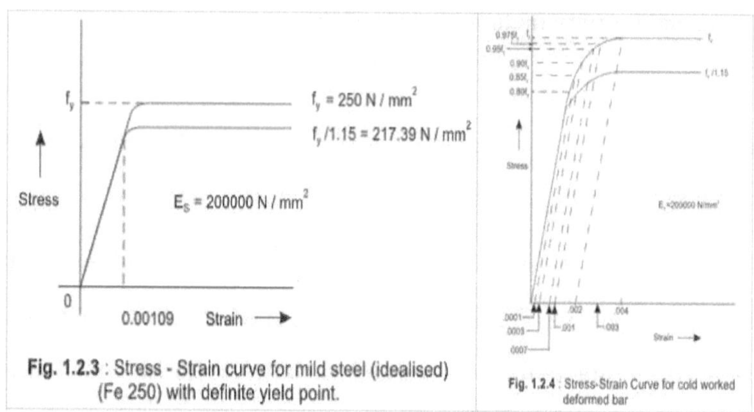

Fig. 1.2.3 : Stress - Strain curve for mild steel (idealised) (Fe 250) with definite yield point.

Fig. 1.2.4 : Stress-Strain Curve for cold worked deformed bar

## Partial safety factors for Load:

The factor by which characteristic load value are increased is termed as partial safety factor of load.

**Design load = (partial factor of safety) x (characteristics load)**

Value of partial safety factors $\gamma_f$

| Load combination | Ultimate limit state | Serviceability limit state |
|---|---|---|
| 1) Dead load & live load | 1.5(DL+LL) | DL+LL |
| 2) Dead seismic/wind load<br>　　a) Dead load contributes to Stability | 0.9DL+1.5(E2/WL) | DL + EQ/WL |
| 　　b) Dead load assists overturning | 1.5(DL+E2/WL) | DL+EQ/wL |
| 3) Dead, live load and Seismic/wind load | 1.2(DL+LL+EQ/WL) | Dl+0.LL+0.8EQ/WL |

DL-Dead load, LL- Live load WL- Wind load EQ- Earthquake load

## "APPROACH OF A SUCCESSFUL ENGINEER"

Author: Himanshu,
Assistant Professor,
Department of Electrical Engineering,
Jind Institute of Engineering and Technology, Jind (126102) Haryana.

The approach of an engineer is very important as it decides whether he will be successful or not in his carrier. The approach of a successful engineer includes the following points:'

### 1) Don't be hesitant to pose inquiries and learn

In the cases that you are experiencing issues in classes or can't sort out the situations that are being determined on the whiteboard; request that your teacher clarify it once more. Most teachers truly want their students to learn and grow. They often complain that their students seldom pose inquiries.

### 2) Read, read and read various books

A few course books attempt to explain troublesome material by giving practical examples and simple clarifications. Look at those pieces of your text assuming you're having inconvenience rather than simply looking for solved examples that resemble schoolwork problem. Read everything in your library and all the other things that you can get help you with your course work.

### 3) Work with your classmates.

At the point when you work alone and get stuck on something, you might be enticed to quit, where in a group study somebody can have a solution to your problem. Working in gathering may likewise show you preferred ways of tackling issues over the manner in which you have been utilizing. Explain all solved problems to all individuals in your group prior to finishing a study session.

### 4) Make your portfolio.

You may have a very busy timetable yet can attempt to take an interest in each experiential learning project you can get your hands on. This will assist you with applying the information that you gain in college and also you will have a portfolio that you can you show in your job interview.

### 5) Build a decent network of connections

Engineering is certainly not a separated field however requires authority and teamwork. You want to construct your own network connections in college so that you are not lost when you start your profession. The most effective way to build network is to have great associations with your classmates, seniors, teachers and alumni. Attend seminars, conferences and meetings organised in your college. Make the best use of online media to keep in contact with your network connections.

### 6) Consult specialists

While doing engineering work, the engineers run into problems, as they all do incidentally, so they are counselled by specialists. Aside from your course teacher, counsel teaching assistants, colleagues, other educators who teach similar course, classmates who have recently taken the course.

### 7) Summer Internship

The most ideal way to hold your insight is through useful practical experience so engineering students should do internship in summer when ever provides opportunity. Employers always prefer fresher's students with practical hand on experiences. Likewise, make your portfolio of completed projects. Interning will likewise assist you with getting ready for the new semester!

### 8) No Single Formula

Like best designing issues, there's no single calculation to follow. For any case, there are some "Best Practices" to follow and some Bad Practices to avoid. Furthermore we can judge utility from fun observation. Try not to commit every mistake by yourself; instead learning from other experiences is much better approach for a good engineer.

### 9) Defining Success

There are some of the questions which must be answered. These are

1. Do you have desire to become really rich?

2. Do you have a desire for a job with decent pay?

3. Do you have the intent to change the world?

You may have a engineering career of 15-20 years ignoring these questions, but finally you have to answer these questions and start approaching for success according to your own definition of success.

## 10)  Starting your Engineering Career

Ask yourself what you are passionate about? Do that. Simple capability will not trump your real passion. Getting everything rolling In Engineering. Track down your place of most elevated influence. Match your abilities, interest to what world needs and needs. Your responses will change with time. Allow your profession to advance and can find career value in any kind of work. Simply accomplish remarkable work regardless of the errand. Appear to be chatty? What numbers of individuals you know are doing it? It's generally a decision you make, not intrinsic ability or IQ.

## 11) Which job is best for you to take?

Have a vision of 25 years ahead and think; which advance technology are generally strong/promising? Which line up with your own conviction framework? It may be guard, medication, shopper, corporate, scholarly world. Of enduring position possibilities, which have best groups? You will advance more from associates than elsewhere. Try not to stress over being thought about (horribly) to them. They began very much like you. Deal with your profession; however don't constantly hover over it. Work really hard and a large portion of your vocation deals with itself.

**12) New businesses versus Huge Corporations**.

It's good to do both as your engineering career progresses. New companies are best when you're youthful: additional time, more energy, less to lose. New companies can at times change world drastically. However, most fall flat and generally have less stability. Large organizations have more chances to change world gradually. Recall that those augmentations can accumulate after some time. They set principles. More steady, yet some of the time that likewise implies stifling. Both can be invigorating, and both can very baffle.

**13) How to get hired?**

- Factors deciding are:

- Do you put stock in the mission?

- How remarkable is the group?

- How well the company is running?

- Would this position influence your assets yet request scholarly development

- Geology, neighbourhood culture, place-to-bring up kids, life partner's excitement and finally think about compensation, rewards, stock, benefits.

Be careful "which company likes you best". In Some company you may have experiences like; couldn't eat, couldn't rest, detested works so don't join those and judge yourself which is best for you.

### 14) Practicalities in getting hired.

- Standard guidance proliferates.

- Spruce up, be on schedule.

- Actually take a look at books and sites

- Staff suggestions do matter

- Try not to fail the medication test

- Attempt to address all questions

- Be careful "great at everything"

- Your new manager can't turn that into benefits

- New recruiting bunch has explicit requirements

- Get your work done

- Plan keen inquiries

- Know rudiments about organization

### 15) Your First Engineer Job

- Regardless it is, become best in world at it

- Try not to disguise or add to hierarchies

- Anticipate 2-3 years to settle in and being productive

- Work hard as hard as possible

- You are setting your own standing and direction

- Just High-Flyers have selection of choices for next project

- Track down tutors and good examples (don't battle peacefully)

- Never let your team down in any circumstances.

- Know when to persevere versus which fights aren't worth battling

- Settle in for remarkable work.

Raises normal individual of entire group

In conclusion, have confidence in yourself and don't surrender to any problem.  With hard work and good approach you will become a successful engineer.

## LEGAL KNOWLEDGE AND ISSUES FOR THE ENGINEERING.

Author: Dr. Jagjeet Singh,
Assistant Professor,
Department of Management Studies,
Jind Institute of Engineering and Technology, Jind (126102) Haryana.

1. **Workmen's Compensation act 1923,**

This Act was made in the year of 1923 in India for protecting the rights of workforce working in an organization. This Act was made specially to protect the workforce and providing them compensation in case of any accident or injury while working in the organization, whatever is was working time or extra time duty performed by the employee for the organization. This Act covers all kind of employees like Workers, Managers, Office Staff, Teachers and Other Staff.  The Workmen's Compensation Act 1923, also providing a helping hand to the engineering workforce in all manners. If the engineering workforce is well aware to this Act, then they can easy protect their rights. They can ask any kind of compensation from the organization for their injury or accident. This Act also protects the rights of the family of workforce after death. With the help of this Act the family or the nominated person can get the compensation from the side of Organisation in against of the death their relative or family member who was working in a particular organization.

This Act specially, helps the civil engineering labours, whom are always working in a risky zone,

**Issue for Engineering regarding this Act:** the very first issue regarding this Act, is that, the labour has not more knowledge for the rights protected by this act. Secondly the engineers some time face problem from the side of upper level of management, because some time they don't get much support to protect the rights. And lastly for getting the compensation with the help of this act, the engineers and other labour working on a project has to pay some extra amount to follow the Government Procedure for getting Compensation through this Act.

2.  **Payment of Wages Act 1936**

In the year of 1936, the Parliament pass the bill of Payment of Wages for the Employees. Payment of wages Act was made for the protection of the rights of employees in case of extra and unnecessary deduction in the wage or the salary of employees.

If any organization, whatever it is registered or non registered according to the norms, has not pay the complete amount of salary or the wages of the employees then in that case the employees can report against the organization for unnecessary deduction in the salary or wages and can get the full or complete amount of their right.

Most of the time, most of organizations make an agreement with the employee at the time of joining the job in the oraganisation, that they will show a high amount in the documents in the form of salary or wage but always pay a lesser amount to the employees. This kind of behaviour is completely illegal and reported as under criminal offence according the Payment of Wage Act 1936.

All kind of employees can report their issue regarding unnecessary deduction in the organization under this Act.

**Issue for Engineering regarding this Act:** The very first, the engineers also work under the guidance of the organization and in that case they can't even protect their own rights then it is very difficult to assume that they will helping in the protection of the rights of the engineering labour working in an organization.

Secondly, the engineering labour has not more information about legal procedure for documentation.

One of the major issue faced by the employee or engineers for getting accurate Payment of their work, that at the time of their Joining the Job, they has not signed the document or they has not read the terms and the conditions of the working of the organization, carefully.

3. **Minimum Wage Act 1948**

In 1948, The Indian Parliament has defined a 'living wage' for all employees I India, for the level of income for a worker and employee which will ensure a basic standard of living including good health, dignity, education, comfort and provide for any contingency. However, it was keeping in mind an industry's capacity to pay the constitution has defined a 'fair wage'. And Fair wage is that level of wage that not just maintains a level of employment, but seeks to increase it keeping in perspective the all industry's capacity to pay.

India introduced the Minimum Wages Act in the year of 1948, giving both the Central government and State government jurisdiction in fixing the wage amount. The act is legally non-binding, but statutory. Payment of wages below the minimum wage rate amounts to forced labour is punishable according to this Act.

**Issue for Engineering Regarding this Act:** Most of issues are faced by the engineers to get the wage and Salary of their own and working with them. The first and the major issue faced by the engineering workforce id that they don't have proper information about their actual wage or salary according to the norms and working condition offered to them by the oraganisation, and even they know then they don't have proper information to protect their rights according to this Act.

It is h big issue for the engineering workforce to decide and fixation of the wage rate, most of the organizations following the wage rate chart made by their management or higher authority, but in most of the fields, the Government predefines the Wage or Salary Rate for employees and workers which have to pay to them by the oraganisation.

4. **Payment of Bonus Act 1965**

The Payment of Bonus Act 1965 provides for the mandatory annual payment of bonus on wage and salary to eligible employees of establishments which employ twenty or more than twenty persons. In accordance with the terms of this Act, each and every employee who draws a salary of Rupees 10,000 or below Rupees 10000 per month and who has worked for not less than 30 days in the organization in an accounting year, is eligible for getting bonus (calculated as per the methodology provided by the Act) with the floor of 8.33% of the salary or wage payable to the employee and a cap on the maximum bonus amount statutorily payable (20% of the wage and salary). The Amendment Act for the Payment of Bonus Act also raises the calculation ceiling for payment of the bonus and retrospectively places the onus on the employers to make payment of bonuses to all the eligible employees effective from 1 April 2014.

**Issue for Engineering Regarding this Act:** The Major problem faced by the engineering workforce, is undecided rate of salary or wage on which the payment of the bonus has been awarded to the employees. One another issue, also faced is, to justify the working days and hours of the employee because most of the organizations are not maintain the daily attendance record or the employees.

5. **Equal Remuneration Act, 1976**

Equal Remuneration Act, 1976, provides guidance for the payment of equal remuneration to all men and women workers are working in any kind of organization, it prevent the of discrimination made among the employees on the ground of sex, against women, in the matter of providing and engaging them on the Job. This Act provides the guide lines for payment of equal wages to all for same work and similar nature to all male and all female workers and also for not making discrimination on the basis and against female employees in the matters of transfers, training and promotion etc.

**Issue for Engineering Regarding this Act:** First of all, most of the Engineering staff doesn't have proper knowledge about the meaning of the Remuneration and for what purpose and where this work can be used. And a Less number of women engineers are working and also not well aware with the rules of the Act and guidelines for getting equal remuneration from the organization. The women employees are working in the field of engineering does not have any experience in the field of Law and Professionalism, That's why they are always cheated by the organization for offering and the payment of the Equal Remuneration.

### 6. Industrial dispute Act 1947

The Industrial Disputes Act was made to secure industrial peace and the harmony by providing machinery and procedure for all investigation and settlement of the industrial disputes by negotiations in nature. This Act is covered under VII chapters and 40 sections for settlement of disputes. It is applicable in the whole of Country. The Act came in to force on the 1st April, 1947. The Act provides the settlement of disputes in between workers or employees and the management. The Act currently does not apply to those persons who are employed in a supervisory kind of capacity. In this Act the term "Workman" is defined under Section 2(s), of The Industrial Disputes Act, 1947, "any person (including an apprentice) is employed in any industry to do any type of work such as manual, unskilled, skilled, technical, operational, clerical or supervisory work, are to be, for hire or reward, in the terms of employment be express or implied is treated as the Employee of such organization.

This act is very useful for the engineering workmen for solving the dispute. With the help of this Act Engineers can protect their rights from management and also help the engineering workforce for smooth and effective working.

**Issue for Engineering Regarding this Act:** The miss-conception is in the mind of engineering workforce because they assumed that this Act is only for the workers and the management but it covers all the employees whatever they are engineers, clerks or other supporting staff, working with the engineering on a particular project or industry.

7. **Contract Act 1872,**

**"An agreement enforceable by law"** the definition given in the Law.

For making anny kind of contract in india, there is an Act and which is known as Indian Contract Act 1872, this act was passed in the year of 1872 before independence of the country and same has been followed to current time for making any contract.

The Indian Contract Act 1872 is as it is used in Pakistan before Independence of the both of Country but there are some amendments was made in this act time to time in both countries.

For making a contract, there should be minimum two parties and have their mutual consent to perform or to do some work or assignment. All Contracts are treated as Agreement but all Agreement will not be called as Contracts. For making a contract, first of all an Agreement, which is in the form of written, is necessary and it should be legal.

This Act was enacted on $25^{th}$ April of 1872 in India by Imperial Legislative Council.

### Issue for Engineering Regarding this Act:

There is also one miss-conception regarding this Act is that, is is also a part of Law or used for the managerial and industrial smooth operations but it is very important for the Engineers to make successful the Project activities. Without knowledge of this Act, an engineer cannot make any agreement or contract as a necessary activity of any assignment. In most of the cases, engineering workforce will be hired by any organization without any legal consent or making contract, or a legal contract. It is necessary to appoint an employee, worker, deal with other party or suppliers, the engineers have to know about this act and performed their duties according with the guidelines of this Act.

### 8. Employee's State Insurance Act 1948,

The Employees' State Insurance Act, 1948 was a social security law that provides the medical care and cash benefit in the form of contingencies of sickness, maternity, disablement and death, due to employment injury of the workers while working.

The Allowance for unemployment is equal to 50% of wage/ salary for the maximum period of up to Two Years. Medical care also for the employee and the family from ESI Hospitals/Dispensaries during that period. There are also provisions for Vocational Training for upgrading skills of the employees and the Expenditure on fee/travelling allowance borne by ESIC.

**Issue for Engineering Regarding this Act:**

The issue faced by the engineers for regarding this Act, that they work under uncertainty and because of family burden and other responsibilities and that's why the employer take the advantage of their, responsibilities' week point and not providing any kind of social security and even the engineers also not forced the employer to provide the ESI benefits because of the risk to leave the job.

9. **Payment of Gratuity Act 1972,**

The Payment of Gratuity Act, 1972 was made in India, the law that makes for industries to pay a one-time gratuity to all retired employees. The law applies to the railways, ports, factories, oilfields, plantations, mines and shops. The gratuity is 15 days' wages or salary for every year of employee's service or partial year over six months to be paid to employee.

Gratuity is payable only if an employee have been with the employer for a period of five years or more. But this rule is waived if any employee dies or is disabled, superannuation, retirement or resignation from job. In such cases, the gratuity is to be paid to the nominees or to the employee, even if the tenure of service is less than 5 years.

In Gratuity, the Interest payable at the rate of 8% per annum by the employer, only if the payment is made within four weeks, but if failing then with rate of interest would be payable at  10% per annum.

**Issue for Engineering Regarding this Act:**

Most commonly, the engineers switch their job before completion of the period of five year, and that's why they are unable to get the benefits under this Act. If an employees work more than five year continuously then the employer has to pay the Gratuity amount to the employee or worker.

10. **Sexual Harassment at Workplace (Prohibition, Prevention and Redressal) Act 2013**

The Sexual Harassment of Women at Workplace (Prevention, Prohibition and Redressal) Act, 2013 is a known as legislative act in India that seeks to the protect women from sexual harassment at their official place of work. It was passed in the Indian Parliament on 26 February 2013.

It covers Every organization, whatever public or private, and having more than 10 employees, and should be committed to provide all employees, a safe and congenial work environment and ensuring that they are not subject to any form of the sexual harassment.

Further, every organization should endeavor to create secure working environment for all persons whom are engaged for organizational activities by management. Every employee should enjoy his or her working environment and that will be free from all forms of harassment, like and including sexual harassment, any unlawful discrimination, and the intimidation while working for the Enterprise.

**Issue for Engineering Regarding this Act:** In most of the organizations, the senior employee or the management always take undue benefit of the women employees because of any of their need. While working on any project or assignment the engineers have to move from one place to another and in the situation of Women engineer, it is very hard to work in such conditions and because of these conditions they have to compromise with some issues and after that the chances of harassments will increase. And in the rural areas the women engineers also has not enough knowledge to protect their rights, from any illegal activity.

**Some others Acts relating to the working with and as an engineer**

**Income Tax Act 1961**, it helps the engineers to decide the taxable amount on the overall income gained by them from all sources.

**Employee Compensation Act 2009**, it provides a helping hand to all engineering workforce to get the compensation according to the set norms of the Government and by the Law.

**Maternity Benefit Act 1961**, this Act helps the women workers, employees whom are working as engineer or on other job profile can get the maternity benefits provided by the Law during the period Pregnancy and for a specific period after the delivery. The act clarifies all rules and regulation in this regards in detail for all Government and Public Sector or Private organizational Employees.

**Employee's Provident Fund and Miscellaneous provision act 1952**, the Act Guide about the deduction and contribution made by the employer and employee from a part in his or her salary in the account of Employee named as EPF. A fixed percentage will be contributed by both employers as well as employee is necessary. It is for the long term saving and the amount will be utilized by employee after a fixed age period.

**Common Issues:** These Acts or Laws are a part of service of the employee, but while working as engineer, an engineer does not focus on such actions or facilities provided under these Acts for future saving and uncertainty conditions, basically these are also a part of engineering but most of the engineering workforce has not pay any attention on these.

**References:**

- https://www.policybazaar.com/corporate-insurance/ articles/workmens-compensation-act-1923/- :~:text=The%20Workmen's%20Compensation%20 Act%2C%201923%20was%20made%20to%20 offer%20compensation,an%20accident%20during%20their%20employment.&text=Therefore%2C%20the%20employers%20are%20obligated,demise%20or%20disablement%20during%20employment.

- https://paycheck.in/career-tips/women-paycheck/women-legislation/payment-of-wages-act-1936 - :~:text=The%20Payment%20of%20Wages%20Act,delay%20in%20payment%20of%20wages.

- https://clc.gov.in/clc/sites/default/files/MinimumWagesact.pdf

- https://clc.gov.in/clc/acts-rules/payment-bonus-act - :~:text=The%20Payment%20of%20Bonus%20Act,of%20 8.33%20percent%20of%20wages.&text=3%2C500%20per%20month%20and%20the,3%2C500%20per%20month.

- https://www.indiacode.nic.in/handle/123456789/1494-:~:text=India%20Code%3A%20Equal%20Remuneration%20Act%2C%201976&text=Long%20Title%3A,connected%20therewith%20or%20incidental%20thereto.

- https://labour.gov.in/sites/default/files/THEINDUSTRIALDISPUTES_ACT1947_0.pdf

- https://legislative.gov.in/sites/default/files/A1872-09.pdf

- https://www.esic.nic.in/Tender/ESIAct1948Amendedupto010610.pdf

- https://labour.gov.in/sites/default/files/THE PAYMENT OF GRATUITY ACT%2C 1972_0.pdf

- https://en.wikipedia.org/wiki/Sexual_Harassment_of_Women_at_Workplace_(Prevention,_Prohibition_and_Redressal)_Act,_2013-:~:text=The%20Sexual%20Harassment%20of%20Women,at%20their%20place%20of%20work.&text=It%20was%20passed%20by%20the%20Rajya%20Sabha%20(the%20upper%20house,Parliament)%20on%2026%20February%202013.

- https://www.incometaxindia.gov.in/pages/acts/income-tax-act.aspx

- https://prsindia.org/billtrack/the-workmen-s-compensation-amendment-bill-2009 - :~:text=The%20compensation%20to%20employees%20in,90%2C000%20to%20Rs%201.40%20lakh.

- https://labour.gov.in/sites/default/files/TheMaternityBenefitAct1961.pdf

- https://www.epfindia.gov.in/site_docs/PDFs/Downloads_PDFs/EPFAct1952.pdf

# ACCOUNTING: A STUDY AND RESPONSIBILITY.

Author: Dr. Jagjeet Singh,
Assistant Professor,
Department of Management Studies,
Jind Institute of Engineering and Technology, Jind (126102) Haryana.

The accounting is returned in well-known and contemporary monetary statements. The consequences of all transactions arising over the amount of the accounting length are summarized for and the record, income statement and coins float statement. The monetarystatements of massive companies are audited yearly with the assist of an outdoor CPA company. For a few, like agencies which could be offered publicly, trying out are often a crook requirement. However, creditors frequently require the consequences of an annual outside audit as a neighborhood of their credit score rating agreements. Therefore, pinnacle agencies can also have annual audits for a couple of reason.

In this Study we have Considered Introductory part about the Financial Accounting and its Commercial Developments. Accounting is that the system of recording a billboard enterprise transaction associated with a billboard enterprise. The accounting includes summarizing, reading and reporting such transactions to monitoring agencies, regulators and community organizations. The monetary statements utilized in accounting are the accounting approach throughout accounting, summarizing the enterprise's overall performance, monetary overall performance and coins flows.

It conveys the results of business company to diverse stakeholders, owner, lenders, investors, authorities and diverse organizations. Although accounting is often associated with  the buying and selling commercial enterprise, it is now not the most convenient buying and selling entity that creates use of accounting. people that like housewives, officers and other people who use accounting. for instance , a housewife need to preserve a report of all of the cash she has earned and used. he can write his coins receipts on one net website of his "own circle of relatives diary" whilst checking out many such things as milk, food, clothing, house, school, etc. Such a file will assist him to:

(i)    Investment assets and objectives

(ii)   That his receipts are quite his money owed or vice versa?

(iii) Balance of surplus or deficit, if any at the peak . Three during a state of affairs duringwhich the housewife appreciates her transactions regularly, and further can get essential records approximately the type of receipts and bills. for instance , he need to get the whole quantity he spent on time (say year) for lots such things as milk, food, school, entertainment, etc. , items from relatives, etc. Therefore, at the peak of the bulk (country the year) he can see for himself what his monetary state of affairs is, what he has and what he owes. This will assist him plan for the destiny and his benefits (or make a budget) on a far large scale.

The want for accounting is virtually too fantastic for somebody to behavior commercial enterprise. You would like to know: (i) what are his belongings? (ii) What does he owe? (iii) Whether to form cash or lose a buying and selling commercial enterprise? (iv) what's his or her monetary recognition indicating whether or not or now not she or he could be prepared to

Perform all his or her responsibilities for and the on the brink of destiny or for and the system of monetary conversion.

American Accounting Association (AAA): AAA defines an "Accounting method as a system of acquiring and measuring monetary records to allow knowledgeable judgment and selection via way of means of records customers."

According to A.W. Johnson: "Accounting is often described thanks to the chain, integration and recording of monetary transactions, the exercise of monetary critiques, the assessmentand interpretation of these updates and as a outcome using those statistics critiques and controls".

Weygand, Kieso & Kimmel: "Accounting as a records system that identifies, realizes and transmits organizational monetary instances to the clients concerned."

This definition of accounting thoughts as a records system that identifies real-time transactions verifies outcomes  and presents statistics to the various customers concerned once in a while in an easy-to-use or standardized manner for his or her needs. Basically accounting isn't usually an audio system, may be a statistics tool or a practical tool to provide statistics to clients who've an interest in measuring their picks.

**Description of Accounting**

The essential purpose for accounting is to make earnings or loss to some time , to position financial hobby for and the commercial enterprise on a given date and to possess the electricity to defraud enterprise assets. Such monetary statistics are supplied to preserve commercial enterprise transactions and to alternate the statistics to be utilized  by management, commercial enterprise proprietors and therefore the diverse stakeholders. Accounting may be a machine for recording, sorting, summarizing and specifying financial statistics nearly during a drag sport to make clever picks which may be possibly worrying. The American Institute of Certified Public Accountants defines monetary accounting as "the assignment of recording, classifying and summarizing for and the utmost essential and systematic phrases of monetary transactions and offerings partially, now not below finance, and describing the consequences of that". The American Accounting Association defines accounting as "the  system of  identifying, measuring, and  sending  monetary statistics  to permit knowledgeable choice and use of real-time users. The next are the subsequent accounting requirements:

Recording: its ready recording the transactions of monetary transactions during a scientific manner, presently follows their increase for and the energetic Financial Records.

Separation: another systematic take a glance at of recorded data for the rationale of trying to find identical transactions during a single place.

This drawing is finished with the assist of bookkeeping for and the occasion of a huge big variety of cash owed for and the corresponding games.

Summary: is prepared the schooling and presentation of time-separated data so one can gain users. This diagram includes the schooling of the 5 economic statements alongside the Statement of Benefit, the record, the Statement of Changes for and the Financial Position, the Economic Performance Statement, the Useful Statement.

Translation: Nowadays, the above 3 abilities are advanced with the assist of the usage of virtual processing devices and consequently the accountant should consciousness on accounting aspects. Creditors need to interpret long-time period statements during a logical manner. The accountant need to now not be capable of provide a specific rationalization of what happened

**Accounting policies**

Accounting Regulations name for precise accounting ideas and techniques for the utility of those ideas observed with the assistance of the usage of the commercial enterprise in preparing and finishing economic statements. Policies are supported with the help of employing a selected idea of accounting types, guidelines and agreements. Accounting necessities issued with the assistance of working accounting companies are restricted and restricted to the number to which the accounting guidelines for commercial enterprise length help and commercial enterprise transaction reporting could also be decided.

Therefore, excellent accounting ideas are decided with the assistance of working the commercial enterprise according with the usually usual accounting ideas and necessities. for instance , for and the equal sense, a lower need to be taken thanks to the very fact the proceeds of doing commercial enterprise are blended with the proceeds of the equal period. As beneathneath Accounting Standard-6 it is also calculated with the help of using line type, written for and the form of an honest cost, consequently, the employer desires to construct arecord on what technique to follow. Similarly, asset valuation, interest treatment, subsidy length, constant asset fee etc. they're crucial areas that need the recognition of accounting guidelines to form sure the value and reliability of data.

### Use of accounting calculation

The preceding segment in recent times highlighted the importance of data. Functionalchoice involves accurate, dependable and well timed information. The want for cost and excessive pride of data varies with the importance of the picks with the intention to be made for and the knowledge of that knowledge. The subsequent sections observe to diverse customers of economic information and what they are doing there with the knowledge. People can use economic information to regulate their famous problems alongside the usage of and managing the cash owed in their economic institutions, checking the suitability of an employer's employment, making an investment, renting a house, etc. Business managers need to set dreams for themselves, examine upgrades and cause corrective moves for and the context of principal deviations from the intentional motion path. Account information is required for lots such options - tool purchases, storage, borrowing and lending, etc. Therefore, they're going to be curious approximately acquiring monetary information from an organization that they're going to be brooding about making an investment in. Economic statements are crucial to the availability of data submitted for and the organization's annual evaluation and to diverse monetary papers and journals. Public and administrative authorities feature a duty to regulate our social and monetary device during a manner that promotes social inclusion. For instance, the Securities and Exchange Board of India (SEBI) compels the employer to reveal excellent monetary information to the sponsoring community.The authorities' mission of managing the economic financial system machine will subsided difficult at an equivalent time as economic data alongside profits, expenses, taxes, etc. it's supplied internally for and the equal manner besides for unreliable home windows or 'sports'. Central and meantime governments pay diverse taxes. The tax authorities, consequently, become given to direct the sale of the organization to calculate the number of tax the organization become given to pay. The knowledge created with the assist of accounting enables them in those records and detects any escape attempts. Workers and exchange unions use economic information to unravel diverse problems related to salaries, bonuses, allocations, etc. data enables decide whether or not the organization is for and thetechnique of charging or exploiting customers, whether or not the businesses display superior commercial enterprise overall performance or now not . , whether or not America, a is experiencing an economic decline, etc. which they're carefully related to our complete life.

## Accounting - accounting instruction

Accounting could also be worthwhile to a degree as it is supplied through the size of the inputs and outputs and, as an outcome, offers a foundation for measuring the general performance or overall performance of the enterprise. The dimensions approach is employed to assign numerical values to make a decision symbols or gadgets decided in gadgets or events. Access to property, prison responsibility or different capital need to be interpreted in phrases of publicity to monetary devices with enough reliability. Prices are towards the benefits of products, energy or ideas. Balance may be a monetary idea. The value is to use a monetary device for and the form of money that enjoy its use. Within the calculation of a coin, a unit of ford is leased at a charge, expertise or idea. The truthful cost is measured financially. If the precise cost of the tool is taken as 2, 00,000, it is simply one among the utmost famous expenses alongside acquisition or cost. Measuring an extensive view is true fomeasuring. The thought of equation consists of equation. Typically, four length bases are normally recognized for and the accounting scale eg

(i) Historical Costs;

(ii) Current Costs;

(iii) Actual expenses; and

(IV) Current Value.

**Historical Costs:** Means the acquisition charge, i.e., the acquisition charge of the acquisition.Debts are recorded for and the experience of the number earned at the alternate  in demand.

**Current Cost:** Assets are carried on the worth of coins or coins equivalents which will be charged on a cutting-edge date or equity. Debts are deducted from a payment or comparable quantities of money that permit you be required to pay a cutting-edge requirement.

**Virtual cost:** within the experience of size, objects are recorded in coins or coins equivalents that permit you be obtained via the way of disclosure for and the regular course. Similarly,the number owed is recorded of their reimbursement amount.

**Current Value:** within the view of this cost, the asset is taken into consideration for and the discounted profits balance that the asset is anticipated to provide for and the regular operation of the buying and selling enterprise. Similarly, liabilities are disclosed within the quantity of coins glide this is often required to pay the prison liability for and the regular or suitable duration of enterprise activity.

Understanding between accounting and responsibility

Although the functioning of Acting and Accounting is certainly utilized in another manner however there could also be little line of branch among them. Term of employment of Accountant for drawings of accountants-accountants and professional persons. Accounting is ready for 6 transactions of all transactions which will be adjusted and ready for and the form of quite one money owed and monetary statements. And it is a totally unique area like economics, physics, astronomy etc.

## Accounting Works

Accounting is one among the utmost critical sports activities in nearly any commercialenterprise. It's frequently controlled financially or through an accountant for the duration of little company, or for and the form of giant  monetary departments with many personnel in huge companies. Reports generated within side the form of the many accounting streams, alongside accounting and monetary control, are critical in supporting managers in making knowledgeable enterprise and enterprise decisions.

## Key types

• Without a buying and selling enterprise scale, accounting  could also be a be counted of decision-making, monetary planning, and monetary overall performance.

• An accountant are often capable of lookout of straightforward accounting requirements, however a licensed Public Accountant (CPA) wishes to be used  for giant or large accounting activities.

• Two critical sorts of commercial enterprise accounting are accounting and monetary control. Management monetary control assists regulatory groups in making enterprise enterprise decisions, on the equal time as pricing enables buying and selling enterpriseproprietors decide what number of a product wishes to be charged.

• The subsequent accountants hold a tough and fast of Generally Accepted Accounting Principles (GAAP) whilst making correct monetary statements.

Financial statements summarizing the general performance of an enormous company, the function of coins and its sluggish transferring time are brief and included updates that assist the monetary liabilities of the corporate. As an outcome, all accounting appointments are the previous outcome of years of visibility and rigorous trying out blended with constrained yearsof monetary accounting experience. While simple accounting talents are used for and the form of a bookmaker, excessive accounting is usually considered for and the form of licensed public accountants with positions along side Certified Public Accountant (CPA) or Certified Management Accountant (CMA) inside us. In Canada, the names of three sites - accountant (CA), licensed General Accountant (CGA), and authorized ManagementAccountant (CMA) - are covered below the Chartered Professional Accountant (CPA) line.

**References:**

• "Financial Accounting - Definition from KWHS". The Wharton School. 28 February2011. Retrieved 13 July 2018.

• "Who We Are - January 2015"(PDF).IFRS.org. IFRS Foundation. Archived from theoriginal (PDF) on 1 May 2015. Retrieved 28 April 2015.

- IFRS Conceptual Framework (2010) Par. OB2

- ^ European Accounting Association, Response to Question 26, Comment Letter to the Discussion Paper regarding the Review of the Conceptual Framework, on Page 2 of comment letters, dated 2014-01-24 Archived 2014-07-29 at the Way back Machine

- ^ "IAS 1 - Presentation of Financial Statements". Deloitte Global. Retrieved May 9, 2017.

- ^ Larry M. Walther, Christopher J. Skousen, "Long-Term Assets", Ventus Publishing ApS, 2009

- ^ Gavin, Matt. "GAAP VS. IFRS: WHAT ARE THE KEY DIFFERENCES AND WHICH SHOULD YOU USE?". Harvard Business School Online.  Retrieved 2 November 2020.

- ^ Malhotra, DK; Poteau, Ray (2016). Financial Accounting I. AcademicPublishing. ISBN 978-1627517300.

- ^ Fred., Phillips (2011). Fundamentals of financial accounting. Libby, Robert., Libby, PatriciaA.(3rd ed.).Boston: McGraw-Hill Irwin. ISBN 9780073527109. OCLC 457010553.

- ^ Paul H. Walgenbach, Norman E. Dittrich and Ernest I. Hanson, (1973), FinancialAccounting, New York: Harcourt Grace Javonovich, Inc. Page 429.

- ^ Cost and Management Accounting. Intermediate. The Institute of Cost Accountants of India. p. 17.

• Buchheit, S.; Collins, D.; Reitenga, A. (2002). "A cross-discipline comparison of top-tier academic journal publication rates: 1997–1999". Journal of AccountingEducation. **20** (2): 123–130. doi:10.1016/S0748-5751(02)00003-9.

• ^ Merigo, Jose M.; Yang, Jian-Bo (2017). "Accounting Research: A Bibliometric Analysis". Australian Accounting Review. **27**:71–100. doi:10.1111/auar.12109. ISSN 1835-2561.

• ^ Swanson, Edward (2004). "Publishing in the majors: A comparison of accounting, finance, management, and marketing". Contemporary Accounting Research. **21**: 223– 255. doi:10.1506/ RCKM-13FM-GK0E-3W50.

• ^ Korkeamäki, Timo; Sihvonen, Jukka; Vähämaa, Sami (2018). "Evaluating publications across business disciplines". Journal of Business Research. **84**: 220– 232. doi:10.1016/j.jbusres.2017.11.024.

## LEADERSHIP QUALITY OF ELITE ENGINEER

Author: Kanika,
Assistant Professor,
Department of Management Study,
Jind Institute of Engineering and Technology, Jind (126102), Haryana.

### Leader

An individual who can improve the performance of a particular work by providing proper guidance to a group of person and creates an inspiration for future with a vision and motivates them towards that vision. He encourage the people to form a team and work with proper coordination to achieve their goal by encouraging them. A good leader must have clear focus, honesty, integrity and a clear vision.

**Leader:** Showing up their skills on time to meetings and turning in work on schedule with thoughtfully.

**Engineer**

When a person uses scientific knowledge to design, invent, construct, and maintain a variety of machines. They are expert in their fields. They implement their analytical skills in an efficient and methodological way in order to solve a problem efficiently where you can solve your problems, exactly you can say is engineering. Engineer have all the answers to the problem with well-defined logic and reason.

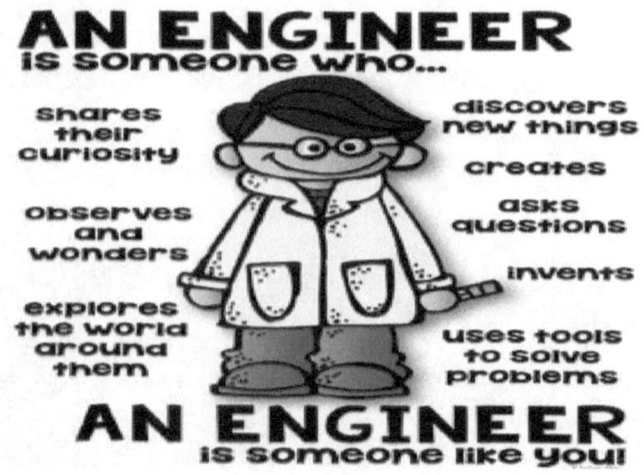

### Leadership In Engineering

Engineeringcannot be completed without leadership quality because when engineer gives practical shape to his idea he need a group of person to complete the goal because of scientific skills and analytical skills involved in their work.  It is not possible to design or construct and getting things done all alone. To be successful, engineer must work with others in a team. To manage that team you must possess the quality of a good leader. For example: An Engineer wants to design a mobile then he needs experts in different field for software update, making of prototype, test phase and packaging etc. Manufacturing doesn't mean that putting the pieces together it involves a long process that involves more than one individual.

So, an engineer must have qualities of a good leader to give practical shape to his ideas. Without this quality final product may lack one or more quality and manufacturing process will become more costly.

So, for the success of engineering carrier an engineer must have qualities of a leader. We will discuss all the qualities of a good engineer leadership in detail.

## LEADERSHIP SKILL IN ENGINEERING:

- Appraise Risk and Taking Initiative. This focuses on analytical and decision-making techniques.

- Delivering on Time in situation of Obstacles.

- Prolificity and pliaibility.

**Engineering Leadership skills**

Leadership plays a vital role in the success of the team. Leader manages the humans who manages the machines. Important skills for an engineering leaders are:-

- Building Relationships

- Problem solving

- Thinking clearly

- Communicating clearly

- Managing their team with responsibility

- Action oriented mindset

**The Responsibilities of an Engineering Leadership**

Each engineer leader has own capability and focus on own set of responsibilities.*Leader* coordinating multiple direct reports, teams or department. It follows:

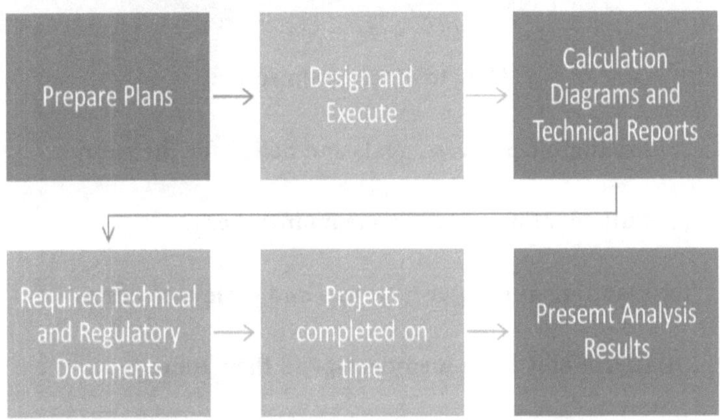


An engineering leadership responsibility cannot describe in one line but responsibility can be divided in to following categories:

**(i) Manage Teams:** Engineering leader not only manage their work but also create corporation among them by checking their capabilities by using analytical skills and assign work accordingly. For Example: Leader set a goal and assign work to an individual according to their specialisation, not giving work to a team. So everyone will be happy and will make team together with great enthusiasm.

**Team manager should ability to carry out and coordinate a team to execute their tasks and common goals.**

**How to direct team spirit:**

(a) **Intelligible purpose, goals and belief for the team**

(b) **Build confidence among team members**

(c) **Planning at regular intervals and review meetings**

(d) **Direct how team membersspend their time**

(e) **Empower their team regularly**

**(ii)        Manage Projects:** Engineering Leader have a control on the activities of the team people, so that they can recognize any problem and issue or change if needed and making them understand the project specifications ensuring that work will be on time and accurate.

**Basic process to manage a project from start to end:**

**Types of Leadership in Engineering**

In Engineering more than one way are found to lead their teams. Most important approach of leadership on engineering, we are discussing below.

**(a) Autocratic**

*Autocratic leadership* is a leadership where one person controls all the activities and takes very few ideas from other group members.

**Benefits**

- Takes quick decision-making especially in stress-filled situations

- Clear view

- Works well where leadership is required

**Drawbacks**

- Depresses group input

- Hurts morale and leads to acrimony

- Ignores creative solutionsand downgrade other group members

**(b) Democratic**

***Democratic leadership*** is a type of leadership where the leader makes decision with the idea of team members based on the everyone on the team.It is a very free leadership style that includes eachmember of the group in the decision-making process. It boosts the morale of each employee. It balances a cooperative spirit that motivates the team and improves the morale of the group.

The main characteristics of democratic leadership are:

- **Encourage the members to share their creative ideas:** The leader asks and expects the members of the group to provide better inputs for the job.

- **Engaged group members:** The leader involves members and encourages them to provide the better solution to become involve others.

- **Boost confidence:** The leader gives a chance to his subordinates to feel free for the job and build confidence without supervision.

- **Gratifying creativity:** New ideas are reinvigorated and rewarded.

In this all the team participation is given importance leader takes input from members who gives time to time report and think on it. Individual feels free to give opinion, raise voice, speak out their problems and speak out and create innovative ideas. This type of leadership style suited where urgent decision is not required. This approach will best suited where all the team is fully experienced.

This approach is best because recent study shows that participation of subordinates becoming must. Modern approach says that more responsibility lays on subordinates more responsible they will feel about their work. They will feel an integral part of the management and this will boost their confidence.

### (c) The Laissez-faire or Free-rein leadership

The Laissez-faire leadership is an approach that allows and gives freedom to others to individual/any worker to make their own decision.

This approach restricts any power and responsibility of the leader. The leader permits the authority and responsibility to  subordinates to make their decision and takes a less participation in administration. He stretches no input, no order and agrees them to establish its own point of view for solving problems.

The leader/trailblazer role is minimum. He comes with the idea that when he left, it does not affect the idea because each member of the group will give best efforts for the job.  In this it is assumed the when a person gives more responsibility despite of strict control and supervision he will perform better with more motivation. But there is no control no supervision, the organization can be flounder.

### (d) Patriarchal Leadership

*Patriarchal leadership* is an approach that necessitates a leading authoritative personality who thinks as a father of the team. Leader is a one who lead the team and behaves team like a family (give respect to each member of the team) and the leaders expect trust, obedience and loyalty from the employees of the family.

**Advantages**

- Leads to increase in productivity

- Boost employee morale

**Disadvantages**

- Take time away from performing

**tasks and goals**

- Clash of personalities

Under this management style leader relation with their subordinates are like a father or paternal. Paternalism means papa is always right and have perfect knowledge. Father always cares for his family like this leader cares his subordinates by providing them better working conditions and fringe benefits it is assumed that good working conditions and gratitude will create motivation among subordinates. They will work harder for the fringe benefits. This leadership style was successful in Japan with her social background.

But this style is not so effective in small farms of india. This approach does not apply on matured adult employees, many of whom have better knowledge and does not like to be looked after.

**Skills needed to be an engineering manager**

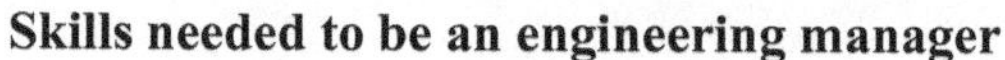

An engineering leadership requires a thorough understanding of their technical skills to make them understandable to others. They must have capabilities to make understand others and solve the problems on time on large scales. They have full responsibility on their head to provide Directions to team and this becomes critical to stay on the date for recent research.

Here are some traits of leadership needed for a good engineer:

**(a) Problem solving**

An engineer must have capability to solve a problem with different angles. An engineer try lots of effort to solve the problem with every angles from whom he/she can provide best solution for that problem.

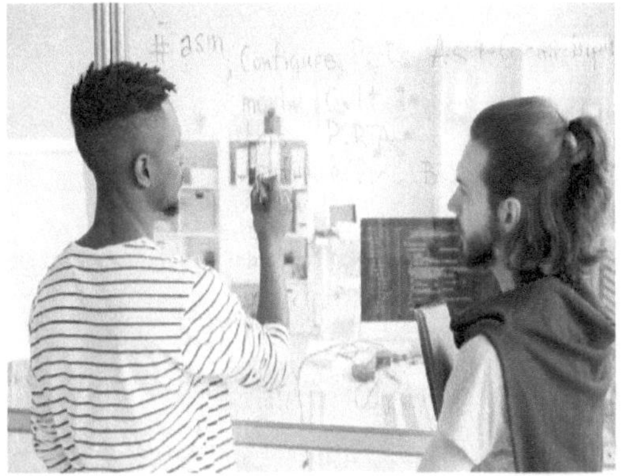

People have to solve their problem with interact with each other and give better results as compare to individual thinking.

Leaders need to able to challenge themselves and succeed when conditions are not favourable.

### (b) Collaboration

Collaboration is an important part of engineering and for team work. Steps of engineering is not complete alone, so as a leader in this field, it's essential to stimulate a team or department that works together.

This figure shows collaborate their knowledge with each other and gives best output. In team work collaboration is an important part.

They must have ability to engage colleagues to thoughtfully work towards a single goal.

### (c) Diligence

As a leader managing multiple direct reports, group or departments keeping the entire organization on track is key. That means being punctilious about deadlines,project milestones and quality standards-while also staying on the top position.

### (d) Strategy

It can be easy to become too concentrated on the day-to-day grind and make sure that every procedure is on time.  However, good leader keeps an eye on their team success for the long term and seek towards smarter approaches.

### (e) Communication

Additionally imaginative and original solutions, the leader needs to convey the reason behind the decision they made and procedure being implemented. Share your goals and achievements in your department with other leaders that can open your team up to new resources.

Communication skills is a very important part of leadership quality. *Communication skills* are the capabilities you use when giving and receiving different kinds of information.

## (f) Emotional Intelligence

It might not be the best quality of an engineering leader. Yet, it is important to have capacity to engage with those who will be influenced by your work, whether those are the members of your team or clients and end users.

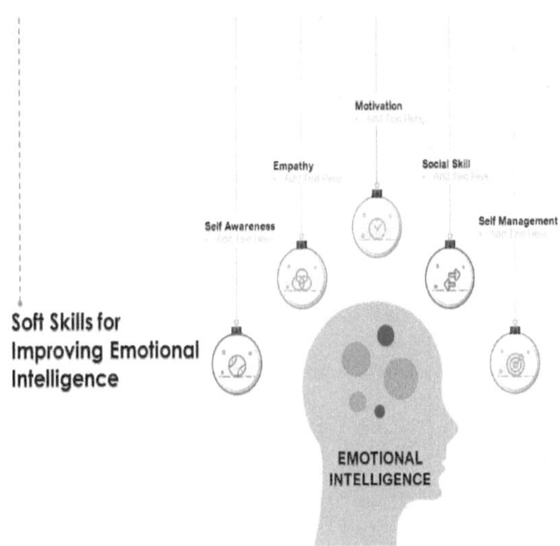



Emotional intelligenceis the capability to understand and lead your own emotions. It is important for part to get success in life. Leader who stays in control and calm is an essential for success.

**Five elements for success in life**

1. Self-awareness.

2. Self-regulation.

3. Motivation.

4. Empathy.

5. Social skills.

Robust&effective leadership is necessary to run businesses smoothly in every industry. There is no exception for engineering.

- **INSPIRES OTHER**

When a group includes personnel with better leadership qualities, optimum utilisation of resource allocation, personnel projectsit results as an overall improvement. Leaders, with their maximum efforts to producebest work and inspire others.

- **EXAMINING RISK AND TAKING INITIATIVE**

Calculate risk and take initiative is vital in all leadership roles, including engineering.

- **DELIVER PRODUCT ON TIME DURING CONSTRAINTS AND OBSTACLES**

Engineering Management courses lay the footing for planning and organizing, and provide tools and methods to develop a range of management decisions to cover all bases.

**Technical Supervision**

A technical supervisor is a professional who interactsthe technical personnel members in a software IT company. They work for software engineering teams and troubleshoot technical.

A technical supervisor needs to have a deep professional knowledge in software development and a clear perceptibilityof technology, but he will also capable enough to  lead a team and collaborate with others effectively.

**What is Technical Leadership?**

Technical leaders think about making astonishing products and the best engineering teams. He always works for his team and his team members. These leaders are also motivated and highly interested in the explanation and full concept. Their precedence is on teams' happiness and output by clarifying out noise and errorless allocation.

### Why Technical Leadership Is Important?

#### Hiring

It is important to have best engineering talent to technical leader, but so is diversity and inclusion. A functional team is a team that scrutinized whole views and points.

#### Motivation

A leader teaches through example to their team. In technical leadership, perhaps more so than other fields of leadership, it uses the concept from bottom to up: to team being a servant, solve their problems by working side-by-side with them to help them and fulfil their dreams.

#### Scale

Engineering leaders ensure their team is productive. They protect their team from any distraction and interruptions and wishes while making fruitful decisions. This empowers the group to work with full capacity and allow business to reach on heights

Technical lead vs. Engineering manager

A technical leader is responsible for serving their team members on the technical parts of their jobs, such as coding, programming and execution. They also explain new projects to their team and troubleshoot any glitches that occur during formation their products. In contrast, an engineering manager is more focused on supervision their employees. They are accountable for business growth and team targets.

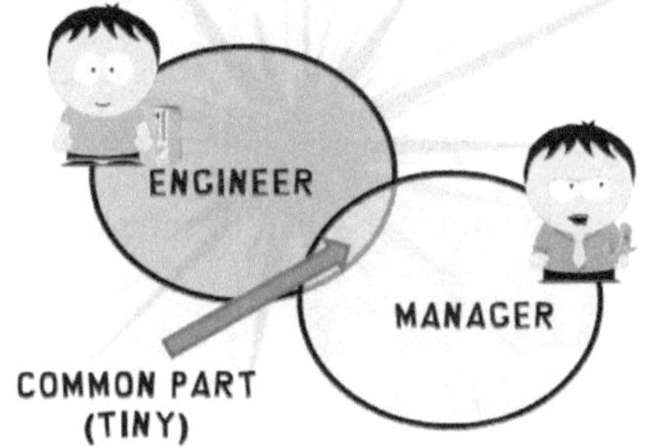


As an engineering manager, you need to have excellentmanagement skills and be able to evaluate your team's long-term goals, while you are likely to work proactive and focus on day-to-day tasks as a technical lead. Only a few portions become common from where they need a special skill and patience to manage both leadership.

How to become a technical leader

If you bearing in minda career as a technical, here are some steps you should follow:

α) Graduation

β) Pursue certification

χ) Develop essential skills in technical field

δ) Increase professional knowledge

### a) Graduation

Most companies hire a technical professional require a degree in an applicable field, such as computer scienceand Information Technology etc. During pursuing your education, focus on coding, troubleshooting and technological skills. You can also join appropriate organizations that focus on particular areas where you nurture up your career. You should be done an internship in a technical industry to gain experience and knowledge while you complete your degree.

### b) Pursue certification

Certification is necessary to go ahead in a technical world. One certificate is done that may improve your chances of being hired for a leadership position. A certification entails for advanced career growth.

### c) Develop essential skills in technical field

During professional experience, work on increasing your skill for this job. Here are few skills that can help you become a more competent technical lead:

- **Technical knowledge**

A technical leadershould be a strong technical abilitylike coding, programming and working on computer systems, security principles and scripting. Gain maximum knowledge about software development and computer engineering. By improvising these skills, you can become better at managing technical problems.

- **Leadership**

Impressive leadership skills to encourage and guide your team members is needed. As a technical leader, it is your duty to persuade everyone remains productive and gets projects done within time or before time.

- **Communication**

Much of your job as a technical leader is presenting support and guidance to your team members, so it's important to be able to give clear cut instructions and set much more needed expectations. With a good written and verbal communication, you can persuade that your team understands their obligations.

- **Multitasking**

Employers want a technical leader who can deal many projects at once and presenting innovative products in the market. Focus on improving your decision-making and organizational capabilities to help you efficiently manage your work pressure.

- **professional experience**

Most employers look for technical leader who have experience in software development or other careers opportunities related to computer Engineering. To gain this experience, you can either work within a company to become a technical leader or gain work experience at one organization and then apply for a technical leader to another organization elsewhere. Here are some jobs you can pursue that may help you get a position as a technical leader later on:

- Software Developer

- Software Engineer

- Programmer

- Web Developer

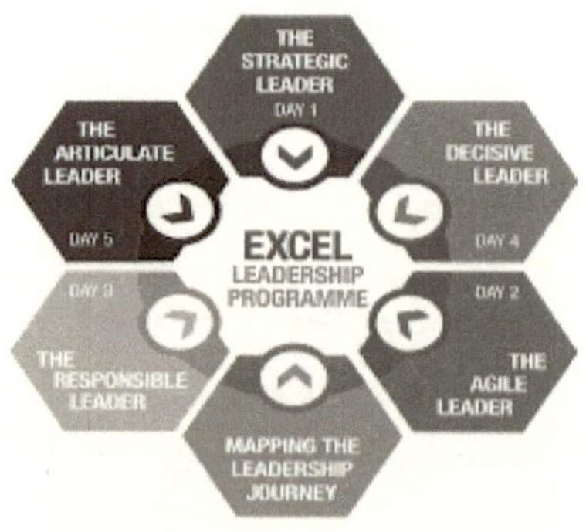


**Programme Leader**

Programme leaders can be**accountable for academic,**

**administration and assessment leadership**, for the programme they have been selected to work. They ensure the effective planning, management and analysisthe programme, adhering to detailed monitoring and evaluation procedures.

## Programme Leadership

*ProgrammeLeadership* provides the tools and procedure needed to meet the organisation's *leadership* challenges and benefit for the company.

## Types of Programme Leadership

## Theoretical leadership

Theoretical leadership is a leadership that includes such as **creating vision and mission** that is based on research for the organization, set up creative ideasand providing teamwork.

Theoretical leadership should practice on

**1.Critical Thinking**

**2.Empathy**

**3.Collaboration**

**4.Flexibility**

**Management Leadership**

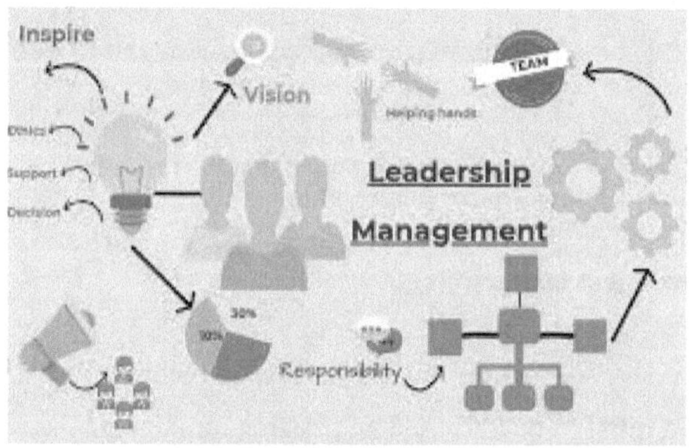


Management consists of **governing a group to accomplish a goal**. Leadership refers to an individual's capability to influence, motivate, and empower others to contribute toward organizational success.

Leadership is primarily a part of directing function of management so it's focussed on some management skills like

α) **Planning**

β) **Organizing**

χ) **Directing**

δ) **Controlling**

## Assessment Leadership

Assessment Leadershipis a **process of identifying and recitation an individual's unique appearances** as they have to lead, manage, and direct others and how such characteristics fit in a given position's requirements.

Assessment Leadership characteristics includes:

- **Candidate's goals**

- **Motives**

- **Feelings**

- **Attitudes**

- **Behavioural tendency**

**Programme leaders** are responsible for creating the programme with appropriate teaching and learning methods, implementing any other necessary modifications, communicating information to team. They safeguard the effective planning and review of the programme. Programme leaders are also responsible for taking to forward any new programme proposals.

**What makes a good leadership program?**

Teamworkis very important for today's leaders. A leader who wants to build a environment for highly interactive programme for his employees and give freedom to his employees to take their own decision.

Leader should provide a coach or a mentor for the team individually. He should also adopt job rotation, project leadership and job shadowing.

**How to Implement a Leadership Development Program**

1. Attach overall program goals to high-level business goals.

2. Plan a journey right for learners' needs.

3. Know your sponsors and get them on board.

4. Manage the tools to help learners succeed.

5. **Think about what fundamentals need to be consistent.**

6. **Build a disposition plan.**

7. **Don't forget about the essential resources.**

8. **Brand a program to connect with learners.**

9. **To make it easy for learners start.**

10. **Measure show value.**

# PROBLEM SOLVING SKILLS-THE ESSENCE OF AN ENGINEER

Author : Neeraj Mor,
Assistant Professor,
Department of Computer Science And Engineering,
Jind Institute of Engineering and Technology, Jind (126102), Haryana.

## Introduction

Engineering is the technique and special knowledge to create and design various projects. Inside the engineering, engineers put their efforts and plans. But they face a lot of problem to create different plans and strategies. They should have some different types of knowledge and skill to solve different types of problems. The solution is depending on nature of problem. Effective management and effective technique is very useful to remove the problems of a product, project, method and type of need any technique.

*"If I had an hour to solve a problem, I'd spend 55 minutes thinking about the problem and 5 minutes thinking about solutions."*

*-   Albert Einstein*

## Contribution of Engineering in Various Sectors:

Mankind has come a long way. From the discovery of fire to the creation of robots - it is leaving no stone unturned to make human life easier. Engineers have a very important role in all these.

The study of engineering is very important in today's time and everyone in this world feels the importance of engineering.

An engineer is one who develops new ways through his scientific knowledge, experiments, inner wisdom and judgment to use material or forces of nature economically for the future of mankind. With his imaginative mind, engineer gives a lot to the society to improve their lifestyle.

Major contribution of an Engineer can be experienced in the fields of the following areas-

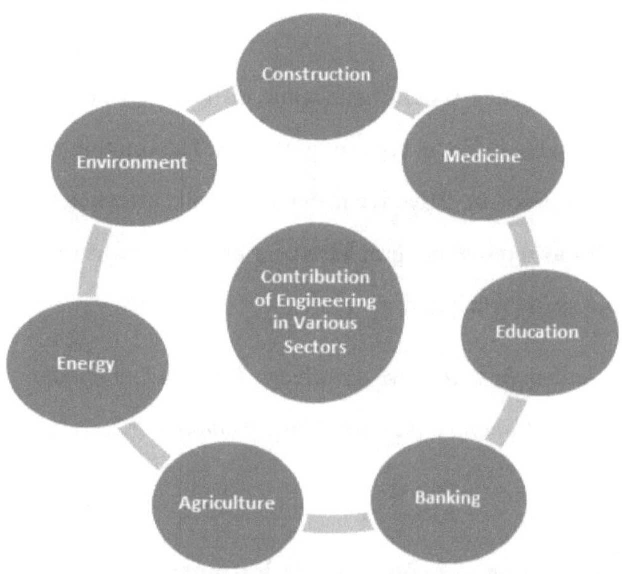


**Figure:1 (Contribution of Engineering in various sectors)**

1. **Construction: -**

It was difficult to build like the Hoover Dam, Burj Khalifa the tallest skyscraper without the contributions of civil engineers. Engineering plays a vital role in the development of infrastructure which is very important for our culture. Good knowledge of civil engineering has enabled us not only to build pools, dams, tunnels, expressways, etc. but also it has found a way to effectively handle traffic congestion, trouble and many other situations.

### 2. Medicine:

When we think about the promotion of medical science, the image of a highly qualified doctor comes to our mind. Engineering and medical science go hand in hand to improve the quality of healthcare, it has contributed a lot in the field of medicine after that we can imagine like MRI, X-ray, pacemaker, stethoscope, surgical instruments etc. All the equipment used in healthcare is made by engineers, all this has been possible only by the principles of engineering.

### 3. Energy: -

Today's era is the age of machines, there is no doubt that at present man himself has also become a machine. Today man has invented such new techniques. Seeing whom we press our fingers under our teeth. Have you ever wondered about the technology that allows small household appliances to reach heavy machines in factories easily and in less time? Such techniques have been discovered by scientists by which electric current is passed through high tension wires at very high speed, due to which many hours of work can be seen in minutes which we cannot even imagine.

How can you be sure that the grid is designed by the engineers? This has been possible only with the help of an electrical engineer. In today's time, we need a huge amount of energy for almost all our work. Electrical engineers design transformers, power grids and commutators etc. Electrical engineers are helping us to get energy by generating electricity. Today all these have increased the power generation even more. Generating electricity has grown at a very fast pace in the last decade. Apart from generating electricity from water, cheap sustainable sources like solar energy and wind power are also being used as an alternative.

## 4. Environment: -

Environmental engineering is the most important sector to improve and control environment related problems. Environment includes our natural resources like air, water, forest, soil etc. All these are the integral part of our life, it is our responsibility to keep them safe. To protect the life of our animals and crops, we have to keep the earth clean by reducing the various types of pollution spread on the land. Environmental engineering helps us in air pollution control, waste management, radiation control, weather management and recycling.

## 5. Education: -

Education engineering is the tool or knowledge about our problem solving skills, building and analysis of complexity, designing and development. In education sector engineering is the important thing to know advancement of technology, system security, economical development etc. Education is the way to manage problems and their effective solution on global level. With the help of education a person can produce a thing very effectively. If we talk about the 21st century the old boring curriculum changed into more convenient for the coming generation. Due to which children are taking more interest in studies and all this is possible with the contribution of engineers.

### 6. Banking: -

Today's banks have become equipped with more technologies and facilities than before. We all think that what is the work of engineers in banks, their field is completely different from that of banks, but the guess is absolutely wrong because today's banks have become very developed and are adopting new technologies, software and all these computers and software are taken care of by engineers only.

Gone are the days when records were made with paper, pen and the work of counting notes was also done by hand which took a lot of time. Nowadays these types of work can be done by computers, also money transactions in banks is done by machines. This is done with the help of software, from which theft and other incidents in banks can also be avoided.

Today engineers are engaged in inventing new technologies to make the banking system more convenient. This will make our future better and safer.

**7. Agriculture: -**

Agriculture is a task to growing something from the land. In involved grains, fruits, vegetables, pulses, jute, cotton, sugarcane etc. With the help of technology a person can grow more crops than usual. Agriculture engineering helps a person in soil preparation, land management, harvesting, plantation, storage. Agriculture engineer can solve the problems of drainage system, irrigation problems, productivity, flood water control and waste management. Many machines are made by engineers to reduce the man power in agriculture.

**Problem Solving Skills:**

Problem solving skill is the tool how to solve problems. Some key skill to solve problems in engineering sector:-

**(1). Communication Skill: -**

Engineering communication skill is very important thing to explain present problems, explain the solution of different types problems put ideas and concept between different types of projects. Communication helps to engineers make plans and implementation of a project. Communication develops understanding between different people in an organization. Therefore Strong communication skill is the powerful tool in collaboration between employers and employees.

**(2). Motivational Skill: -**

Motivation helps the peoples to work efficiently and provide decision making for hard work to employees. Motivation creates opportunity between employees to lead any organization. A motivated person can work and put effort very effectively. Motivation is the key to success in any organization. Motivation can change the view of a person about their work.

### (3). R&D (Research And Development) Skills: -

R & D skills refer to research and development of a product. An engineer should be a good researcher. The knowledge of research and development set a better plan and strategy about market and uncertainty of future. R & D skill helps in solving critical problems, find the challenges in different type of project work, improve communication knowledge and time management.

### (4). Analytical Skill: -

An engineer should have analytical skill with different types of environment like Technological, political, cultural, global, natural etc. Environmental study is very important for an engineer because they effect directly and indirectly to a project. Flexibility can change the whole strategy of an organization. Therefore engineers make policies after analyze the environmental study.

### (5). Decision Making Skill: -

Decision making is very complex in any sector. Before taking decision a person should be make a strategy about future. Correct decision can help to grow any organization. A bad decision may be very harmful for any strategy, because a decision may be effective or not for their customers is depends on decision making during a big project. A decision should be consider customers, government, international market, competitors and different types of environment.

### (6). Leadership Skill: -

Leadership skill is most important in engineering to solve many problems. A successful leader can lead a success company. A leader always supports their team and their company management. A good leader may be a good communicator, locus of control team player, motivator, flexible. A leader always tries to achieve company goals.

### (7). Innovation Skill: -

Innovation refers to adopt a new technology, ideas and concept to achieve their goals of any organization. Innovation is the most important skill to solve business and technological problems by using different types of methods and technology. In various sectors innovation helps in design and creates a new technology.

### Challenges / Problems in Engineering Sectors:

### (1). Identification of Problem: -

In engineering sector engineers of different fields faces many problems during their works. It's very difficult to identify the type of problem at work place. Sometimes organizations identify the problems that is very difficult, we requires special knowledge to identify the problems so that they can be solved and problems arising during the work can be removed.

## (2). Leadership: -

Leadership is the tool to lead and manage a task. But without knowledge and skill a person cannot manage. An organization faces motivation problems, team building, decision making, conflicts, production control and communication. An inexperienced leader never grows their company.

## (3). Technology: -

Technology plays an important role in engineering. In today's era nothing seems possible without technology. Technology is rapidly change and an organization faces challenges from the technological changes. It is very hard to adopt a better technology in any project. The know advancement of technology is very challenging for any project.

## (4). Communication: -

Communication is the most important thing in any field. Communication gap between an employee and employer is very difficult situation to make conversation and collaboration. Many communication barriers come up in an organization like physical barriers, emotional barriers, organizational barriers, language barriers, interpersonal barriers etc. Understanding is a must to remove these barriers.

## (5). Rules & Regulations: -

Rules & Regulations are compulsory for a growing organization. Weak rules and regulations can mislead the real objectives of a organization. Week management is not only for the organization but also for the safety of the public, strong rules and regulation can take the objectives of a company in the right direction. Government rules and regulations also create a challenge for a company or organization. That's why following them is most important, their knowledge is also very important.

### (6). Time Management: -

Time Management means right decision as well as right planning management, production strategy control and implementation. It is as important as planning and once a product is made, it is necessary to bring it to the market at the right time. Poor time management leads our objectives towards failure, so we should take the right decision carefully, for this it is necessary to take the right decision at the right time with the right planning.

### (7). Climate Changes:-

Take any decision keeping in mind the climate changes. Change of climate can be harmful to take any decision without doing climate study in places where it is unwelcomed. Natural disasters can also be the result of climate change, such as earthquake, tsunami, flood, hailstorm, avalanche, dragging mountains etc. It can destroy our infrastructure. Sometimes their study is very difficult. For this, the engineers should have special knowledge and should do full preparation for any climate changes.

**Strategies in Problem Solving:-**

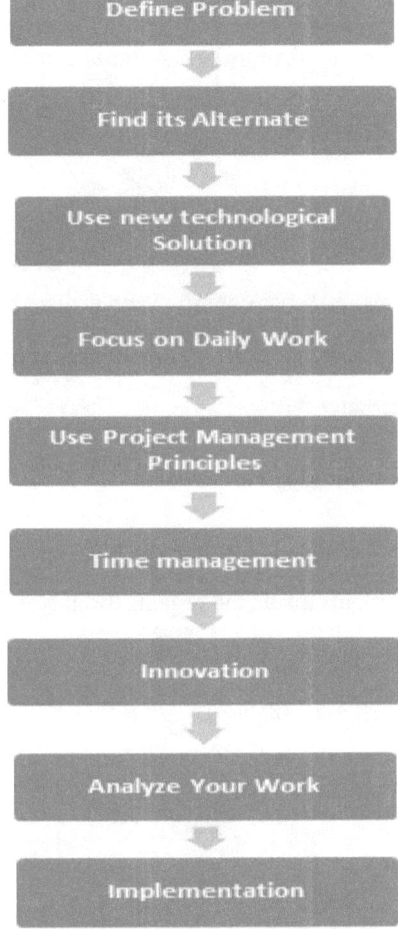


**Figure:2 (Strategies in Problem Solving)**

**(1). Define Problem: -**

Defining the problem is the first step in problem solving. Understanding the nature of the problem inside it, an attempt is made to solve it. Engineers should understand the problems well and bring their brief; only then their solution can be found. When the data of a problem is collected properly only then its best solution can be done.

### (2). Find its Alternate: -

After defining the problem properly and knowing its nature, engineers find its alternatives. The best solution to any problem depends on its nature if it is understood properly. Problem can be any type of land, building, natural or personal. Only after understanding they properly can get its best alternate.

### (3). Use new technological Solution: -

Technology solution means put the technology in business or try to solve technical problems inside the organization. Nowadays technology has become a medium to solve problems and increase production rapidly. In hilly areas, any organization has to face many problems; they can be overcome with the help of technology. There is also a fear of storms and natural hazards in the coastal regions as well. Technology is very helpful in this.

### (4). Focus on Daily Work:-

In this, an engineer keeps an eye on his work by making a chart of his daily, in which the engineer has to prepare a daily plan and see the daily work. In this, all the rules and regulations of management are included, which help in working according to the strategy, like planning, controlling, organizing, managing, leading etc.

### (5). Use Project Management Principles: -

In this, new plans and principles are added according to the daily challenges, which can be changed in the ranking of the challenges and problems of the market. It shows how effective our planning and strategy is and what are the shortcomings in it, according to which they can be overcome. It includes responsibilities, vision, target, rights, standard and feminists.

### (6). Time management: -

All strategies, plans, vision are necessary according to time. Right work at the right time is helpful in achieving the goals of the company. The decisions taken at the right time define our strategy. All types of management can be done only according to the time. It includes stress management, planning, production, technology adoption, cash flow, finance, budgeting and working hours. All these should be managed properly.

### (7). Innovation: -

Innovation means adding new ideas and plans to any strategy. Innovation enhances your values and also improves the quality of the product, keep innovating from time to time. Innovation puts you ahead of your competitors. Time-according innovation increases your profits along with your strategic advantage.

### (8). Analyze Your Work: -

After innovation we have to analyze our work according to

innovation. An engineer has to do a deep study of the principles, process and environment to get the work done unexpectedly. Only after that a decision should be taken whether any changes are needed or not. If there is a time for any change, then it should be changed according to the strategy.

### (9). Implementation: -

Implementation is the last step in problem solving techniques. Implementation means the product has been thoroughly tested and the problems encountered in it have been removed, after that anything can be implemented. This is a very important thing; it will decide the failure and success of an organization's strategy. This will reflect the design, quality, concept, standard of an organization's product.

### Conclusion:-

Engineering is very important thing in any sector. No work is possible without engineering. Engineering has become a medium of problem solving, it is impossible to do any work without it. Technology is being used in every sector. Today, the importance of research and development has increased in every sector, in which the problem of different types has to be faced. Engineering has become a great medium to get effective solution of all this. Today new discoveries are being made for new problems and all this is possible only because of engineering.

# KNOWLEDGE OF FINANCIAL ENGINEERING FOR PERFECT ENGINEER.

Author: Nitin
Assistant Professor,
Department of Management Studies,
Jind Institute of Engineering and Technology, Jind (126102), Haryana.

## Meaning of Financial Engineering

Financial Engineering is a special skill or a professional knowledge of science in which a person can solve the problems and hurdle of day by day financial problems with the help of financial knowledge and analysis of risk management. Inside the financial engineering involves the implementation and formulation of an activity performed by an engineer and an engineer can design & develop new ideas related to finance problems. An engineer should have to some special knowledge of finance and how to manage financial challenges for their projects effectively and efficiently. With the help of financial knowledge an engineer can solve their financial problems in better way.

## Definition of financial Engineering

*Financial engineering involves the designs, the development and the implementation of innovative financial instruments and processes and the formulation of creative solutions to problems in finance.*

*-    John Finnerty*

**Problems in management of finance related for an engineer.**

An engineer face a lot of problems in manages finance day to day work. He can solve these problems with the help of knowledge.

1) **Identification of a financial problem**

2) **Decision Making**

3) **Time management**

4) **Waste management**

5) **Production Management**

6) **Cost Control**

7) **Technological Assistance**

8) **Cash Flow**

9) **Development Challenges**

10) **Maintaince of Machinery**

**(1). Identification of a financial problem: -** Identify a problem of finance is not an easy work. For identify this should be financial knowledge and skill. In an organization or engineering should not be completed without finance. So that financial arrangement is most important at first to run a business or engineering projects.

**(2). Decision Making: -** Decision making process is most important and necessary in any organization or any project. Decision making is a powerful tool of gathering information and identify the problems related to any alternative. In engineering a lot of decisions taken by engineers like –

- Market Policies

- Segmentation

-Buy or Make Decision

- Cost Control

- Production Decision

- Financial Decisions

- Investment Decision

- Budgeting decision etc.

**(3).Time Management: -** When a decision taken by an engineer in any industry or a project time management should be planned and evaluate at any decision. This decision affects the policies and planning of an organization. It is important for future decisions for uncertainty and risk management. Time management provides information about investment and economical perspectives.

**(4).Waste Management: -** Waste refers to the various types of waste at the time of production and handling. For removal this types of waste we should waste management. Waste management helps of an organization to reduce financial problem and recycling of waste things.

Its helps in various types of production and reuse of a product.

(5).**Production Management:** - Production is the base of any organization and any industrial activities. Its start with managerial planning, organizing, directing, controlling and production activities. Production management is a process of converting raw materials into finished goods. In production management financial management is most important tool. It helps in better understanding between a process and the final goods production and it is very useful in waste control.

(6). **Cost Control:-** Cost control is the important tool to estimate cost and maximize profit or reduce cost. When any organization or industry choose any project then they estimates their expenses and profits. For this they make a financial plan for total cost and actual cost. An engineer should be knowledge of this thing. Cost control policy direct affected any decision taken by an organization. Financial decision is most important in cost related decision.

(7).**Technological Assistance:** - Technological assistance refers to those services that provides by preparation, financing and execution of development of a project. A technical engineer helps in technical management in workplace. It helps in operations, production and supply chain. Technical knowledge helps in execution in new technology. For technical support and technical assistance financial management play a crucial role in decision making in new technology adoption.

(8).**Cash Flow:** - Cash flow means is the total sum of amount cash slips as a receipts or distributed amount in financial records. In engineering cash flow show how much amount has been allotted for whole projects of construction or production in a business or industrial activities. It helps in circulating money in right way to whole business activities. It is important for analyze the cost of any activity in particular manner. It is very important any investment by an organization in any activity. It shows the financial condition of an organization in market area.

**(9).Development Challenges: -** An organization always try to explosive growth and worldwide market on global level. But it is not easy without knowledge of finanace and market rules and regulations. Environmental changes, Government Policies & laws of a country, Consumer behavior, Supply chain management, Economies and competitors in market area directly influence in development of a new technology and growth of an organization. So that, market knowledge to a manager is compulsory. Development of an organization is fully dependent on behavior and market analysis of a company.

**(10).Maintaince of Machinery: -** Maintaince of machinery is most important in a working organization. Inside any organization with human work machines is also important for work. Maintaince means keeps the working our machines for production and try to maintain regularly and save it from depreciation. Maintenance of machinery involves regular Maintaince, regular service of machinery equipment, checkup, repairing of machines and timely replacement of non working parts of machines. According to time machine should be change for better production.

**Process of Financial Engineering**

It involves complete life cycle of a product like financial product, statistics analysis, consumer analysis, and programming, testing & launching a product, Innovation etc. These factors affect the procees of a product. It involves financial problems like cash flow, liquidity in market complex market structure etc. So that, any product or technology should be launch according to market environmental condition and analysis of market.

The process of a financial engineering is following below:-

(1). **Identification of Need**

(2). **MVP Creation of a Product**

(3). **Complex Design**

(4). **Product Testing**

(5). **Perfect Product**

(6). **Pricing Factors**

(7). **Marketing of a Product**

(8). **Launching of a product**

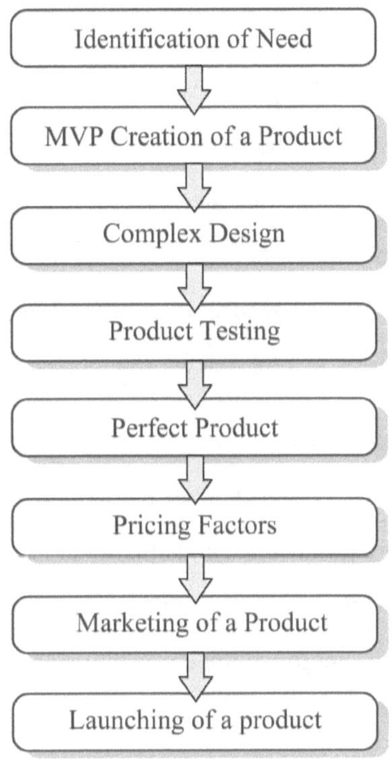


(1). **Identification of Need: -** The first step of this process is identifying the need of a product. In this step an organization find the need and demand inside the market area. For identify the need an organization analyze the market the identify the choice of consumers.

(2). **MVP Creation of a Product: -** MVP (Minimum Viable Product) means a particular product that shows their sufficient features for satisfying the feature of consumer. It is target to satisfy customers to get feedback of their customers. A company has to require this technique to reduce their cost and develop a new product in future for their customers. It is also helpful in remove unwanted risk in development of a product.

**(3). Complex Design: -** When a new product or technology designed by an engineer, he faced much complexity to design a product. For remove this complexity an engineer can get the help of MVP research. Its help to provide feedback of a customer's group. With the help of suggestions and feedback of users designers can remove the hurdles and complexities for a new product design.

**(4).Product Testing: -** Product testing is important to making sure about the quality of a product. With the help of product testing makers want to know their product is a high quality or not. High quality product show that the customer's needs and expectations about a particular product. It is important for engineers design, Parameters, documentation and testing plans.

**(5). Perfect Product: -** Perfect product is a product according to name, design, production style, durability, innovative ideas, quality and customers needs and satisfaction. MVP helps in create in perfect for use. A perfect product can fulfill the desire of society. It shows the endeavor of production team and  management policies success between the market area or customers group.

**(6). Pricing Factors: -** Pricing policies is the element of marketing mix. Before setting a price of any product manufactures include internal and external factors that can affect to a price policy of a product. Some internal & external factors that can affect directly to price decision.

**(A). Internal factors:-**

(i). Market policy

(ii). Market objectives

(iii). Production policies

(iv). Costs

(v). Product Design

(vi). Quality of a Product

**(B). External factors:-**

(i). Customers Needs

(ii). Suppliers

(iii). Market Area

(iv). Transportation

(v). Govt. Policies

(vi). Competitors

After read these factors price of a product may be decided. They are decided to failure or success of a product.

**(7). Marketing of a Product:** - Marketing tool is major concept in success of a product. A strong marketing can help to target end customers. Marketing mix is very important in marketing policies. The fours P's -

(i). Product

(ii). Price

(iii). Place

(iv). Promotion

These factors are decided our market policies is strong or not. They shows about goods & service of a product, actual purchasing power, consumer location according market area and a advertisement of a product. Marketing policy is a tool of communicate with consumers and focus on targets.

**(8). Launching of a product:** - A product launch is a process to introduce a new product to market. In this process manufacturers make a plan to how to launch a product in market. Before launching they decide a date of launching. It is more than important as developing a perfect product according to consumer needs. Launching planning should be effective because wrong launching cannot be attracted customers and make a bad impression between customers in market. So, planning of launching should be very carefully. It is a very critical process. Planning should be start before 8-10 month so that when product is ready for effective launch.

**Conclusion:-**

Financial engineering is an activity of development and problem solving by new ideas and created new instruments for financial efficiency in corporations to solve financial problems. It is very helpful in determine the need of actual finance in any organization. Financial engineering can be developed the financial knowledge and skills in financial engineers. It is most important thing to develop a new product and better customer relations. Customers satisfaction and customer relation helps in grow and innovate a company. Financial engineering also helpful in how to invest, insured and circulation of finance in the market area. Therefore financial engineering play a crucial role in growth in industry.

**References:-**


- https://www.wallstreetmojo.com/financial-engineering/

- https://www.sjf.tuke.sk

- http://www.civil.aau.dk

- https://askinglot.com ›

- https://www.upkeep.com ›

- https://cdn.wallstreetmojo.com/wp-content/uploads/2020/03/ Financial-Engineering-Main.jpg.webp

## CLASSIFICATION OF ENGINEER

Author: Nitin

Assistant Professor,

Department of Management Studies,

Jind Institute of Engineering and Technology, Jind (126102), Haryana.

Engineering does not come in any one field, today engineering is found in every sector along with technology and professional knowledge are require to do any work. Today no sector is untouched by it. We get to see the best examples of engineering everywhere. Evidence of engineering is seen in every corner of the world. Engineering work started when man came into the world, whether it was burning fire or hunting. Man discovered different ways of hunting and lighting fire, he made different types of tools and learned a new art of living. And since then, one after the other new inventions started happening. One after the other inventions have invented new technology and gave a new direction to man. Technology enables man to take effective solutions of new manufacturing problem, economic growth as well as decision making. Technology has contributed in different fields.

**Some different types engineering following here:-**

1. **Civil Engineering**

2. **Computer Engineering**

3. **Electrical Engineering**

4. **Mechanical Engineering**

5.  **Biomedical Engineering**

6.  **Automobile Engineering**

7.  **Agriculture Engineering**

8.  **Aeronautics Engineering**

9.  **Environmental Engineering**

10. **Chemical Engineering**

11. **Textile Engineering**

**(1). Civil Engineering:-** Civil Engineering is a professional qualification that provides assistance in designing, constructing and maintaining any work. Civil Engineering provides construction of many things within such as roads, bridges, railway tunnels, airports, construction of buildings, construction of ports, construction of infrastructure etc. India gate, the Great Wall of China, Tajmahal, Howrah Bridge, Kailas Mandir Temple, Caves of Ajanta and many more is the best example of civil engineering.

There are also some sub-branches of civil engineering which provide extension to civil engineering. Some sub branches are as follows:-

- **Construction Engineering**

- **Site Development Engineering**

- **Transport Engineering**

- **Coastal Engineering**

- **Water Engineering**

- **Structure Engineering**

**Construction Engineering:-**Construction engineering is a branch of civil engineering. Construction engineering is such knowledge that before making any thing, it's planning, style of construction and its management works. The construction engineer is responsible for the one who manages the work and also manages its safety and design. The construction engineer also ensures whether the work is being done according to the plans and time.

**Site Development Engineering: -** Site development engineering is also a part of civil engineering that deals with the management, construction and control of the site. Site engineering uncovers different stages of construction. Site Engineer manages the work on the site, leads the work and maintains the supervision of the project. The site engineer prepares the daily plan and implements it. He manages the day to day work and prepares its report. The site engineer prepares the budget of the work, creates the artwork among the employees and also takes care of the health of the employees at the site.

**Transport Engineering:-**Transport engineering is a function of planning, functioning, design, structuring and operations. Our transport includes all types of transport medium such as airways, roadways, waterways, pipelines, railways and ropeways. They have a great contribution in reaching from one place to another. The job of transport engineering is to make all these mediums safe and effective. Along with this, it also includes economic growth, maintenance of transportation and solving the problems related to them.

**Coastal Engineering:** - Coastal Engineering is also an important part of civil engineering. Coastal Engineering is an important project that involves planning, construction and controlling the need for developing a construction site around the sea with a view to the coast. In this, priority is given to the construction of ports and nearby constructions and the site is developed for their construction. These decisions are taken in view of the ocean, in which disaster management like tsunami, cyclone can be kept safe.

**Water Engineering:** - Water engineering is concerned with preparing the equipment related to the sources related to the management of water. In this, the system related to the supply of water in villages and cities has to be prepared and clean water has to be provided to the people. It also includes managing the flood and rain water in the river drains. Water harvesting is a wonderful example of this.

**Structure Engineering:** - Structure engineering is an important part of civil engineering. In this, a structure of anything is prepared. Its involved color, design, setting up the formation and implementing it. Safety measurement and material selection is very important while making any structure.

**(2).Computer Engineering:** - Computer engineering is a branch of science that deals with the design, construction and maintaince of computers. It would also have been useful in designing computer hardware and software. Computer Science Engineering is very helpful in creating new technology and solving the problems encountered in them. Computer technologies kept coming at different times. So far, different generations of computer have introduced different types of technologies to the computer. The use of networks and technology has made the world smaller, new upgrades have made our work even easier. Internet has extended our reach to every corner of the world. Other areas of computer engineering are: - Processor Design, Computer Network, Mobile computing, Software Design etc. Some sub branches are as follows:-

- **Network Engineering**

- **Software Engineering**

- **Operating System**

- **Coding**

- **Programming language**

- **Machine Learning**

- **Hardware Engineering**

- **Computer Graphics**

**Network Engineering:-**Network engineering is a branch of computer engineering that deals with computer-related engineering networks. A network engineer is a professional who is involved in the maintenance and connectivity of the network with his professional knowledge of technology. Network data can also be in the form of call, video, voice and house hold network. The network engineer also makes sure that the network technology is working properly or not, the same network related plan makes and implements it.

Some types of networks are as follows:-

- **LAN (Local Area Network)**

- **MAN (Metropolitan Area Network)**

- **WAN (Wide Area Network)**

- **CAN (Campus Area Network)**

- **WLAN (Wireless Local Area Network)**

- **PAN (Personal Area Network)**

**Software Engineering:** - Software Engineering is a special knowledge and skill that works to create, design and test any software according to the requirement of the customers. A software engineer is that professional person who designs, builds and maintains the software, when that software is ready, then tests it and removes the shortcomings in it. Some types of software :-

- **System Software**

- **Application Software**

- **Programming Software**

- **Driver Software**

- **Open Source Software**

- **Operating System etc.**

**Hardware Engineering: -** Computer hardware engineering is a technique to research, design, create and testing to a hardware device and components. Computer hardware engineers perform this process and build a hardware device like that memory, circuit, processor, etc. Some types of hardware:-

- **RAM (Random Access Memory)**

- **Monitor**

- **CPU (Central Processing Unit)**

- **Mouse**

- **Keyboard**

- **Printer**

**Electrical Engineering: -** Electrical engineering is the branch of engineering that deals with manufacturing, designing and testing electrical devices. Electrical Engineers are those professionals who design, develop and test electrical equipment and overcome their shortcomings such as electric motors, communication medium, navigation, radar, sonar method etc. Electrical engineers test new electrical instruments, fund the defects in them, develop and improve the method of installation. Plans what will be the process of designing the making of instruments, prepares its budget and prepares the latest technology and short out the problems related to it. Some branches of electrical engineering:-

- **Power engineering.**

- **Control engineering.**

- **Signal processing.**

- **Telecommunications engineering.**

- **Instrumentation engineering.**

**Power Engineering: -** Power engineering is a branch of electrical engineering that deals with connecting devices to each other through electrical devices, generating, transmitting, and distributing electricity. Power engineers a person who ensures the safety and maintenances inside the industrial area. Power Engineer is involved in improving the quality of equipment, maintenance of machinery such as Compressor, Boiler and Generator. Some types of power plants;-

- **Hydroelectric power plants**

- **Coal-fired power plants**

- **Diesel-fired power plants**

- **Gas-fired power plants**

- **Solar power plants**

- **Nuclear power plants**

**Signal processing:** - Signal processing is field of electrical engineering that helps to analyze, modify and decipher the signal. Signal processing is used to modify, accelerate, improve, transmit, store and enhance the quality of the signal. Signal processing is used in the areas of audio quality, speech, radar, sonar etc. Some types of signals:-

- **Digital Signal**

- **Analog Signal**

**Telecommunications Engineering :** - Telecommunication engineering is the process of exchanging information through wires and wireless channels. Telecommunication engineering is made up of computer and electrical engineering, which improves telecommunication as well as creates it. Telecommunication engineers design, develop and maintain communication networks. Which includes internet, satellite, data encryption and fiber, its best example is GPS system which helps people to find the address. Some examples of telecommunication:-

- **Mobile Communication**

- **Broadcasting**

- **Computer Communication**

- **Network Communication**

- **Remote Sensing**

**(4). Mechanical Engineering: -** Mechanical Engineering is a Study of problem solving techniques and principles from design to manufacture of related ideas from the objectives of the Marketplace. Mechanical engineering is a medium to analyze the principles of motion, force and energy. Mechanical Engineers are experts in design and manufacture that can make parts from the smallest of machines to the largest of machines. Mechanical Engineers are capable of manufacturing all types of machines such as Engine, Aircraft, Drives, Machine Parts, Gas Turbine Tools and Robots. Some areas of mechanical engineering:-

- **Combustion and the Environment.**

- **Ground Vehicle Systems.**

- **Heat Transfer, Thermodynamics and Energy Systems.**

- **Manufacturing.**

- **Mechanical Design.**

- **Transportation Systems.**

**(5). Biomedical Engineering:-**Biomedical engineering is a branch of engineering that deals with problem solving techniques and principles related to biology and medical science. Biomedical engineer studies the environment related to medical and biology, and designs, develops, manages, evaluates, and controls the processes related to medical equipment. This includes development of medical technology and development of information system. Artificial Organ, ICU Machinery is its best example of biomedical engineering. Some types of biomedical engineering:-

- **Biotechnology**

- **Biomechanics**

- **Clinical Engineering**

- **Medical Imaging**

- **Neuroengineering**

- **Biomaterials**

**(6). Automobile Engineering:-** Automobile Engineering is the branch of engineering that deals with the design, manufacturing, preparation of blueprints and controlling the manufacturing process of machinery related to automobiles. Automobile engineering is related to vehicle engineering which deals with the production, quality, safety and operation process of the vehicle. An automobile engineer is responsible for the process that deals with designing, developing, analyzing machines related to automobiles. Scooters, motorcycles, auto rickshaws, cars, trucks, etc. are good examples of automobile engineering.

Some types of automobile engineering:-

- **Design Engineering**

- **Manufacturing Engineering**

- **Automotive Engineering**

**(7). Agriculture Engineering:** - Agricultural engineering is a task that deals with research, agricultural products and processes related to agriculture. Under agriculture problems related to irrigation, drainage, flood, growth, production and agriculture environment persist. Agricultural engineers play an important role in solving these problems. Environmental engineers do research, supervised planning and management to make this process happen. Agriculture engineer prepares the system for flood and water control, drainage, irrigation. Some areas of agricultural engineering:-

- **Soil and Water Engineering**

- **Waste Management**

- **Processing or Post Harvest Systems Engineering**

- **Farm Power and Machinery Engineering,**

- **Agricultural Resource Management**

**Soil and Water Engineering:** - Soil and water engineering is a sub part of agricultural engineering which helps in improving the quality of soil and water in agriculture. Soil and water engineering plays an important role in improving cropping, fertilization and management, including crop rotation, crop cover and formation of healthy soil. Some types of soil and water engineering:-

- **Atmospheric Humidity**

- **Gravitational Water**

- **Capillary Water**

- **Chemically Combined Water**

**Waste Management:-** Waste Management Engineering is a technology that works to collect, dispose, manage, organize and recycle waste. Its objective is to create related strategies for environmental impact and recycling of different types of waste. Waste Management Engineer plays an important role in this and deals with related problems. Some important parts of waste management engineering:-

- **Recycling and Composting**

- **Energy Recovery**

- **Treatment and Disposal**

- **Biological Reprocessing**

- **Animal Feed**

- **Landfill**

**Agricultural Resource Management: -** Agricultural Resource Management is an important technology that provides information related to field and livestock to the farmers. Agricultural Resource Management is helpful in planning, research, development, animal health related to agriculture. Some parts of agricultural resource management:-

- **Livestock production.**

- **Crop production**

- **Plant Protection.**

- **Water  resources**

- **Agronomy.**

- **Horticulture.**

**(8). Environmental Engineering**: - Environmental engineering is a branch of engineering that deals with problems related to the environment. Environmental problems include pollution related to air, soil, water and sound, and methods of their technical solution, control and improvement are found in environmental engineering. Environmental engineers do research and find technical solutions for this and play an important role in removing the problems that harm human life and related to the environment. Some Types of Environmental Engineers:-

- **Wastewater treatment engineers**

- **Air pollution control engineers.**

- **Pollution control engineers.**

- **Environmental remediation engineers.**

- **Hazardous waste management control engineers.**

**(9).Textile Engineering:-** Textile engineering is a technique that deals with the design, manufacturing process, coloring and its control related to fabric. Textile engineer is the responsible person who studies and does research related to clothes. Textile Engineers work to design quality and control the manufacturing process of fabrics. A textile engineer decides whether the work is being done according to the principles and laws or not, he does the whole process analytically and implements new technologies. Textile engineering involved majorly two sectors:-

a) **Handloom:-**Handloom is a traditional method of designing and manufacturing a garment which includes saris, cotton fabrics and handloom textiles. In this a traditional simple machine is used for weaving of clothes.

b) **Mechanized:-** Mechanized Textile involves in designing, manufacturing and coloring of textiles with the help of modern machines. Some types of mechanized fabrics are Bed Sheets, Towels, Fashion Wears, Bags and Sleeping Bags etc.

c) **Some Areas of textile Engineering**

d) **Technical Textiles.**

e) **Textile Materials and Performance Evaluation.**

f) **Textile chemical technology.**

g) **Fiber science technology.**

h) **Yarn and Non-woven Technology.**

**References**


- https://www.collegedekho.com/careers/automobile-engineer

- https://en.wikipedia.org/wiki/Civil_engineering

- https://www.bls.gov/ooh/architecture-and-engineering/civil-engineers.htm

- https://www.civil.iitb.ac.in/tvm/1100_LnTse/101_lnTse/plain/plain.html

- https://www.fieldengineer.com/blogs/what-is-network-engineer-definition

- https://www.nsenergybusiness.com/features/newsmajor-types-of-power-plants-to-generate-energy-151217-6004336y/

- https://www.rcrwireless.com/20160720/featured/what-is-telecommunications-engineering-tag31-tag99

- https://www.me.columbia.edu/what-mechanical-engineering

- https://alis.alberta.ca/occinfo/occupations-in-alberta/occupation-profiles/biomedical-engineer/

- https://www.collegedekho.com/careers/automobile-engineer

- https://en.wikipedia.org/wiki/Agricultural_engineerin:~:text=Agricultural%20engineers%20may%20perform%20tasks,results%20and%20implement%20relevant%20practices.

- https://en.wikipedia.org/wiki/Environmental_engineering:~:text=Environmental%20engineering%20is%20a%20sub,protect%20human%20health%2C&text=and%20improve%20environmental%2Drelated%20enhancement%20of%20the%20quality%20of%20human%20life.

- https://www.indeed.com/career-advice/career-development/what-is-textile-engineering

- https://www.googleadservices.com/pagead/aclk/sa=L&ai=DChcSEwj34efClo72AhXKnUsFHUMrDakYABAAGgJzZg&ae-2ohost=wwwgooglecom&cid=CAASERon6q%2Cg8ukZG1TSLaqE0tXR4&sig=AOD64_1odKFyvx7enj59Mhud%29yZG5y_9tA&adurl&ved=2ahUKEwik2tClo72AhU8wjgGHT9yBO4Q0Qx6BAgCEAE

# ENGINEERING ETHICS & CODE OF ETHICS FOR PERFECT ENGINEER.

Author: Prabhjot Kaur,
Assistant Professor,
Department of Management Studies,
Jind Institute of Engineering and Technology, Jind (126102), Haryana

## INTRODUCTION:-

Whether individually or collectively, the actions & decisions taken by any engineer always after keeping

In concern with Engineering Ethics . Generally , ethical issues in engineering are loyalty, risk, conflict of interest, whistle-blowing & many more .But recent growth in Engineering Ethics should be considered .

Generally, the main emphasis of engineering ethics is on treating engineering as a profession & also on society "e responsibilities and duties of engineers which have been already laid down e of ethics.

## MEANING OF ENGINEERING ETHICS:-

The term 'Engineering ethics ' is the combination of two words- Engineering and Ethics. Engineering is defined as how creatively scientific principles can be applied  to  develop structures, machines , processes &make a proper use of them either solely or in a combination .The term Ethics refers to the " ability as well as responsibility to judge his decisions from the context of general wellbeing of the society".

Now we can say that "**The Set of rules & guidelines that engineers adhere to  as a moral obligation to their profession & to the world**". With the passage of time, development can be seen from micro ethical issues towards more macro ethical issues.

Micro ethical issues such as unity, honesty and morality  whereas macro ethical issues such as those concern what will be the impact of Engineering and technology on society? Now a days, proactive approaches got more attention .These approaches unite ethics from early in the process of development of technology and designs of Engineering.

**"The Professional Approach to Engineering Ethics & Codes of conduct "**

- Legal protection of titles, of college degrees, universities often connected with exercising a profession.

- It is often believed that a profession must always be committed to an ideal of serving society and certain moral ends.

- The Work which can be done only by your peers  is the evaluation of professional work and also the judgment that some professional has done his or her work efficiently or not .Because only these people possess the skills  along with knowledge to apply to right standard of judgment.

**What purpose is served by Code of Ethics ?**

Mostly, three main types of engineer's applications and responsibilities are served by this:-

- Upholding some moral values like be loyal, maintain confidentiality& be trustworthy if you are serving or working as an agent to your clients and employees.

- Fulfilling certain obligations towards public like meeting your social responsibility to serve public interest.

**Note:-** Code of ethics of Engineering societies are generally advisory in nature as  these express the values to which engineers are committed. (If you are practicing as an engineer, then you can seek advice from these i.e. how to behave ethically?**)**

Basically, Code of ethics have broader scope as these are guidelines for professional conduct !

**Q. What is the purpose of designing these codes ?**

**Ans.** One of the main reason is to help professionals so that they can "uphold the highest level of ethical conduct& maintain standard of practice ." As well as integrity regarding their professional obligations. There are different code of ethics in different countries for different professional engineering societies .But Do you know what's common in these ? (That basic teachings of what is right & what is wrong along with this the procedure of applying it in decision making process).

**Note:-** That single method which can be used in making judgments by professionals !

## SIGNIFICANCE OF ETHICS IN ENGINEERING:-

"Engineering has a direct & vital impact on the quality of life for all people."

Honesty, unbiasedness, equityare the core characteristics for services which are provided by engineers. Engineers must contribute to the protection of the public health & to safeguard their interest. To help the society , every engineer must follow ethics in a better way such as give equal importance to the rights of others, do not pay any attention to unnecessary problems. Be unbiased & fair in his actions , also by always being grateful towards others.

- The basic purpose of spreading awareness about engineering ethics is to help students in preparing for their professional lives. It will help in developing more clarity in their understanding& what they think about ethical issues.

"What can be the reason of giving so much importance to ethics in Engineering?"

The reason behind this is if we have a code of ethics for professional Engineers, then they can raise their standard for their professional behavior. If you take decisions morally or ethically, usually there are chances of consequences can be severe.

**Some moral issues in engineering:-**

1. **Whistle-Blowing:** - If an employee finds that ethical rules are broken intentionally or unintentionally & can be dangerous for the

people living in society, company &consumers. Of course, whistle-blowing is not unique to engineering but there are many reasons that why is it so relatable in engineering. One reason is that Engineers have specialized knowledge of skills, risks &adverse consequences of certain technologies.

2. **Loyalty:** - As we discussed earlier, this is the moral responsibility of engineers (as it is stated in the Code of Ethics of Engineering Societies) is that every engineer must be loyal towards their clients & employees.

3. **Conflicts of Interest:** - Such situation occurs when an individual's or business entity's vested interest raise a doubt of whether their decision making, actions can be impartial. But in engineering, you can find these in different forms like bribery, accepting gifts.

4. **Safety & Risk:** - One of the major professional responsibilities is ensuring safety. As you know Engineering can be done in various fields like mechanical, civil, chemical engineering. "But also for biotechnology Safety & the protection of human health is a prime concern ".

5. **Environmental Care & Sustainability:-** The core element i.e. protection of human health has long been recognized in Code of ethics for engineers but nowadays attention for Environmental Care &Sustainability is required the most Where Engineering perceive safety as a value ,on the other hand , sustainability was long back seen as a major political issue as well as highly controversial. When without

compromising the ability of future generation to meet their own needs, they successfully attempt to meet their present needs such development is called Sustainable Development.

6.  **Maintaining Honesty & Dignity :-** The guidance should be provided to engineers in regards of maintaining highest standard of honesty & unity .If  dignity & integrity of engineers profession is at stake then he shall never promote this act at the expense of it .They shall treat every person with dignity, equality, respect without any discrimination.

**Some Suggested guidelines:-**

1.  Public Statements shall issue by engineers only in objective & fair manner.

2.  False or misleading representations should never be attempted by any engineer to attract an employee from another employer.

3.  Without Consent, any equipment, office or laboratory facilities shall never be used by any engineer on outside private practice.

4.  The must have commitment from engineers is to improve the environment & to enhance the quality of life.

5.  Engineers shall not compete unfairly with others but they can negotiate contracts for professional services fairly.

6.  Whether facilities are tax-free or tax aided , if this is the case then engineers should not use student services at less than the rates

which other employees of comparable competence are receiving ( including fringe benefits ).

7. Engineers shall continue their professional development throughout their careers, and shall provide opportunities for the professional development of those engineers under their supervision.

### Q. Why Study Engineering Ethics?

**Ans.** Now question arises here is why is it important to study Engineering ethics for engineering students In the past few years , several cases came into light that received a great deal of media attention . Due to all this, Engineers gained an increased sense of their professional responsibilities. These cases create awareness regarding importance of ethics within engineering profession.

"As Engineers realize how their technical work has far reaching impacts on society".

**Note:-** If we talk about result of this increased awareness is that today nearly every major corporation now has an ethics office & the main responsibility of it is to make sure that employees if they are facing any issue such as regarding their safety , any corporate business practice , then they surely have that ability to express their concern .

### Q. What do you understand by Ethics problems?

**Ans.** In simple words, we can say that Ethics problems are like Design Problems .Main hurdle is that these problems rarely have a correct answer at which everyone agrees .The core element of engineering practice is product designing, structure & processes. Design related problem is in terms of what specifications are required like price, performance criteria, involving conflicting ethical principles.

**ENGINEERING ETHICS & OPPORTUNITIES:-**There are always some obligations of engineers towards society, their client & their profession .Engineering Ethics performs an important role in complete development of engineering professional which sets & examines obligations of engineers .With the passage of time , as India is becoming a knowledge economy, it becomes very much important that focus should be on advancement of skills especially those which are relevant to engineering economic environment. More & more fundamentals &prerequisite should be included in ethics of engineering education for students so that they learn about social, political complexities of practices. To make this happen, a major revolution will be including ethics course in the syllabus." This will lead to the formation of ethical engineers taking responsibilities, analyzing & implanting them."Usually the system on which engineer works is real time system but the interface with which engineers has to perform in real time is not provided in classroom bounded education .While receiving engineering education, students always feel afraid of introducing themselves, telling about their goals, future plans etc. although there is no lack of potential &sound technical knowledge especially in rural areas. Through ethical teaching this realization will be possible students will get to know what are the needs & expectations of industry, society from engineers & also work culture of industry, all opportunities which are present globally from day one for them .Code of ethics improve the profile of the profession ,raise awareness about issues.

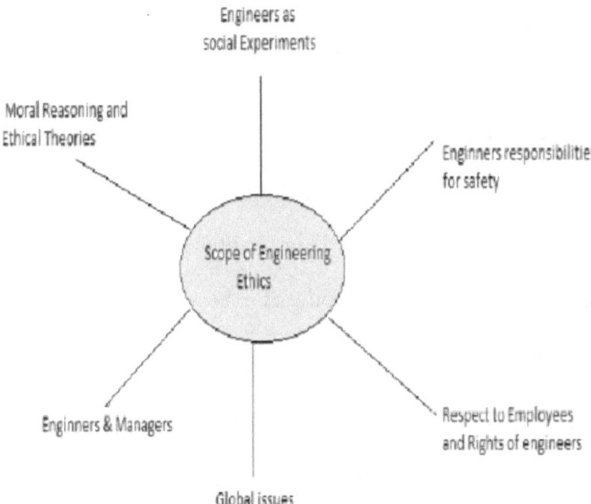


**Figure 1.** Scope of Engineering Ethics

**Figure1.Shows rights of engineers which are included in schematic scope of engineering education.**

Engineers must be aware regarding their right, responsibilities, and roles to be performed as an employee in the development of industry .This may include development from social point of view along with research & development work. Teaching of ethics will provide beneficiary awareness to engineering students about current global issues, impact of these issues on society, responsibilities etc. When engineers will aware about what are the expectations from them only then they will serve in adherence to the highest standards of principles, ethical conduct. To cope up with the current technologies, continuously increasing industrial & social needs, engineering students has to be ethical.

**Conclusion:-**

Engineering discipline is extremely wider in scope & contains a more wide range of specialized fields such as "applied science, engineering & technologies etc." This chapter provides an overview of importance of ethical teaching, code of ethics to cope up with global world challenges, issues etc.

Nowadays, engineering education is not all about taking a degree of 4 years but also to manifest integrity; honesty in their work culture & this will be possible only if ethical teaching is provided at degree level.

# "ENGINEERS, ENTREPRENEURSHIP AND INNOVATIONS"

Author: Radhika,
Assistant Professor,
Department of Management Studies,
Jind Institute of Engineering and Technology, Jind (126102), Haryana

Now a day, engineers are turning into entrepreneurs. Startups and innovation are the new buzzwords. But what makes an engineer a successful entrepreneur? Why the successful startups are owned by engineers? The answer is 'problems'. Yes, the problems that tingle in their mind. They sense the urge a society has. This is the stage where the idea generates. There was a tingle of having a machine that can provide cash twenty-four hours when banks are closed. This persuaded a determined engineer John Shepherd-Barron and his team to invent the machine named ATM.

The times and efforts of going through a lot of restaurants to check the menu and order lunch were huge. Deepinder Goyal, an engineering graduate from IIT-Delhi noticed this. The idea of Zomato tingled in his mind. Deepinder and his colleagues collected the menu of different restaurants & uploaded them on a website. They also provided for home delivery. The startup Zomato bought entirety to the working class. Isn't it entrepreneurship?

**Who is an entrepreneur?**

According to **International Labour Organization (ILO),**

"Entrepreneurs are people who have the ability to see and evaluate business opportunities, together which the necessary resource to undertake them and initiate appropriate action to ensure success."

**Entrepreneurship:**

"Entrepreneurship is the investing and risking of time, money and efforts to start a business and making it successful."

**Innovation:**

The word '**Innovation**' is derived from the Latin word *innovare*, which means *to renew*.

"Innovation is a process by which a domain, a product, or a service is renewed and brought up to date by applying new processes, introducing new techniques, or establishing successful ideas to create new values."

In simple words, entrepreneur is an individual with specific skills and innovative thoughts whereas entrepreneurship is the ability of an individual to convert the idea and the thoughts into reality.

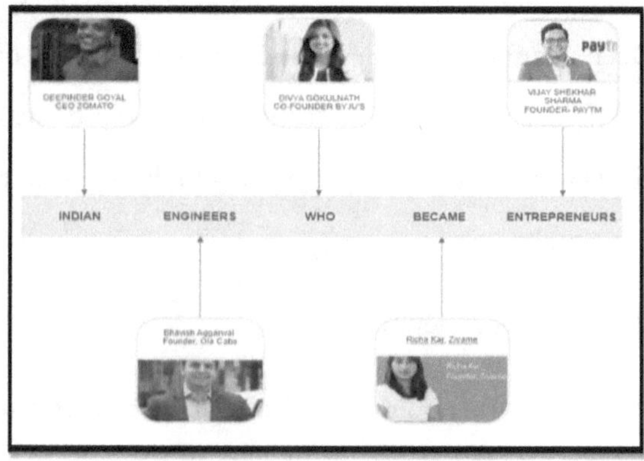

## INDIAN ENGINEERS TURNED ENTREPRENEURS-

As the entrepreneurial culture is at a boom, we can see many engineering graduates around us with unique ideas to launch and run their businesses.

Many of the existing startups are successfully run by engineering graduates. A few examples include Ola, Flipkart, Zomato, Paytm, etc.

### *What motivates them to shift?*

The answer is a unique Idea that could make a great business. They enter the market because they are passionate, believe their product will have a positive impact and hope to make profits from their efforts.

## ENTREPRENEURSHIP QUALITIES AMONG ENGINEERS-

Engineers require technical knowledge but entrepreneurs require soft skills as well. **Mc. Clelland (1961)** highlighted in his book, **"Achieving society"** that successful entrepreneurs are characterized by:

(a) An unusual creativeness;

(b) A propensity of risk taking;

(c) A strong need for achievement.

To become a successful entrepreneur, the following qualities should be imbibed in an engineer:-

1. **Engineers are rational:-** Engineers are more pragmatic in their approach because their subjects are practical. Rational nature helps

them in decision-making for their new ventures.

2. **Enthusiasm for innovation:-** Engineers have a zeal for improving the existing technology. This quality of continuous innovation is what makes them successful entrepreneurs.

3. **Problem-solving attitude:-** An entrepreneur is bound to face various problems regarding the finance, technology, competition, etc. Engineers who have a positive and problem-solving outlook make them fit for the entrepreneurial role.

4. **Sound technical knowledge: -** Engineers have expertise in the technical know-how of their field. This technical knowledge adds to the success of their startups.

5. **Eagerness to learn: -** As machines and technology are prone to become obsolete with time. Engineers who update their knowledge and use this in their innovations have high chances of success, for instance, Google updates its features as per the needs of customers.

6. **Resilience:-** Every business whether small or big faces downturns due to various internal and external factors. Engineers who can withstand difficult times can become successful entrepreneurs.

7. **Risk-taking ability:-** Risk is the sine qua non for the business enterprise. Every start-up includes various types of risks like financial, operational, etc.

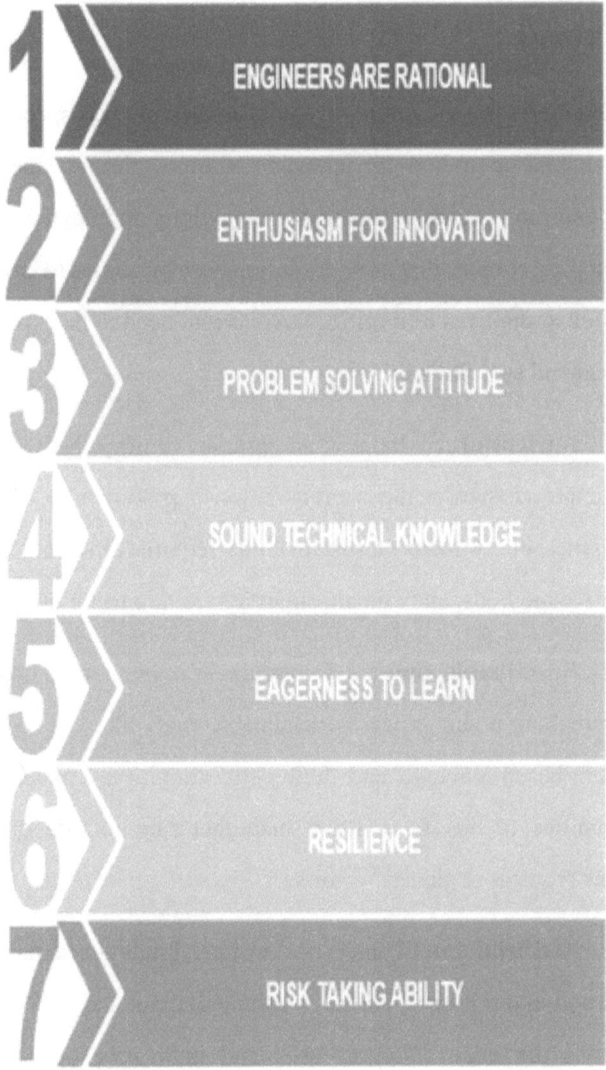


Engineers can become successful entrepreneurs if they possess these basic entrepreneurial qualities.

## ENTREPRENEURIAL OPPORTUNITIES FOR ENGINEERS

Engineers are the future inventors as they possess specialist skills and technical know-how for innovations. Innovation has the potential to add enormous value to practically everything and anything. India is a developing country that provides infinite opportunities to engineers to add value to the lives of its citizen. Areas that need to be explored with technical and soft skills include-

- **Agriculture:** - India is an agrarian country. New challenges like climate change, water shortages, lower productivity, and supply chain issues, etc. A focus on sustainability requires efficient technology, innovative methods, and climate-smart agriculture techniques.

- **Sustainable fuels:** - To reduce emissions from fossil fuels, we are making a shift towards sustainable fuels like electric vehicles, hydrogen-based energy, and fuel cells. Engineers have immense opportunities in this field. From manufacturing to safe disposal of batteries requires engineers' efforts.

- **Artificial intelligence:** - Artificial intelligence has a wider application in our homes, business, administration, and public facilities. There lies the huge entrepreneurial and innovative opportunity for explorations. Artificial intelligence including robotics, the internet of things, big data, and language processing possess tremendous economic opportunities for engineers.

- **Virtual and augmented reality:** - India is like a hungry market for new technologies. VAR technology is at its nascent stage which requires research & development as well as marketing efforts. Don't you think an expert engineer would have a lot of zeal to explore this exciting area?

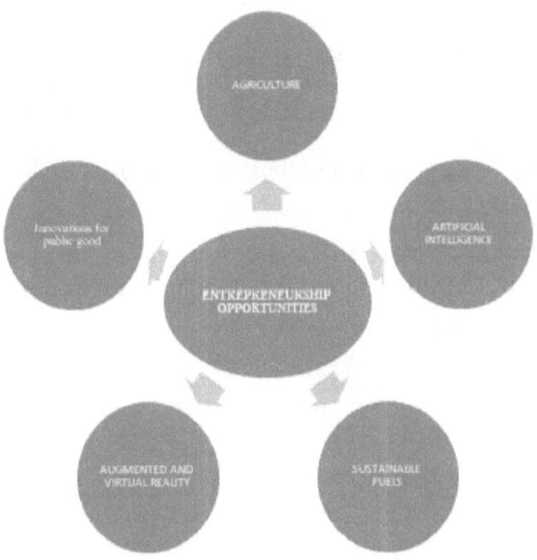


- **Software Development:** - India is the largest supplier of software engineers to the US and many other developed nations. Software engineers are the strategic assets of our nation. Entrepreneurial opportunities in this field are immense like app development etc.

- **Innovations for the public good:** - By and large innovations focus on the needs of the high-income group. But there are underprivileged children for education, physically disabled people, workers with a poor working conditions like mine workers, manual scavengers', etc. who are in dire need of new and cheap innovations. Technopreneurs are coming up with innovative technologies like sensor-based watches for blinds, robots for manual scavenging. But the need for innovations is huge for the 'public good'.

## CHALLENGES OF ENTREPRENEURS:-

Entrepreneurs start their venture with a big dream. To transform the dream into reality is not easy task. Entrepreneurs have to face a lot of problems. Due to number of reasons, sometimes they have to face failures in their startups. Few challenges are as follows:-

1. Lack of Experienced managerial staff.

2. Rapid growth of competitors.

3. Weak marketing strategies.

4. Availability of men, machines and raw material in the country.

5. Poor access to financial resources.

6. More emphasis on short term vision

## CONCLUSION:-

Opportunities available for engineers in the field of entrepreneurship are immense. Engineers with their entrepreneurial abilities fuel the economy. They create businesses that employ people and make products and services that consumer buys. For the success of their entrepreneurial venture, they need to keep an eye on the tingles of society because an entrepreneur turns dreams of society and its future consumers into reality.

# LEVELING ENGINEERING

Author: Ram Mehar,
Assistant Professor,
Department of Civil Engineering,
Jind Institute of Engineering and Technology, Jind (126102), Haryana.

## Meaning of Leveling Engineering

"Leveling is a process to determining relative height or elevation of different points on the earth surface so that it may be used to represent on a plan or map. This is the process dealing with the measurements in vertical plane" as told by Rammehar Kundu.

## Purpose of Leveling Engineering

1.  Leveling is done to determine the undulation of the ground on the earth surface. This is most important for engineers for the purpose of planning, designing and execution engineering projects such as alignment of railways, highways, water supply and drainage etc.

2.  Leveling also becomes necessary in the selection of site for bridges, dams, buildings and sanitary schemes etc.

3.  Setting points in the field to check the heights of objects.

4.  Preparing of contour plans.

5.  To find the depth of cutting or filling for any work.

6.  To find out layout gradients.

**Leveling instruments**

**There are four types of surveying levels:-**

1.  The Wye, or the dumpy level

2.  The Tilting level

3.  Self – leveling

4.  Digital electronic level

**(1).Dumpy Level**:- It is a parts of leveling with the help of this we find many points on the ground and all these points we find reduce level. With the help of this reduce level we plot a contour map any area.

(2)**The Tilting level**:- "A surveying instrument with sighting telescope so mounted that it can be raised or lowered through a limited arc without impairing accuracy of reading, though axis of rotation is not precisely horizontal. The bubble tube is usually mounted alongside the telescope and is viewed from the eyepiece and through an optical sighting arrangement, which either brings opposite halves of the bubble image into coincidence or the end of the bubble to a reference line" by Cobb Duglous.

(2) **Self – leveling:-** "The self-leveling is similar to tilting level except that it has no micrometer screw. Instead, self –leveling level contains an internal compensator mechanism (a swinging prism or pendulum) that, when set close to level, automatically removes any remaining variation from level. This automatically reduces the need for setting the instrument for leveling as in the case of dumpy and tilting level. Self leveling instruments are highly preferred instrument in surveying due to ease of use and minimal rapid set up time consuming" B.C. Punia.

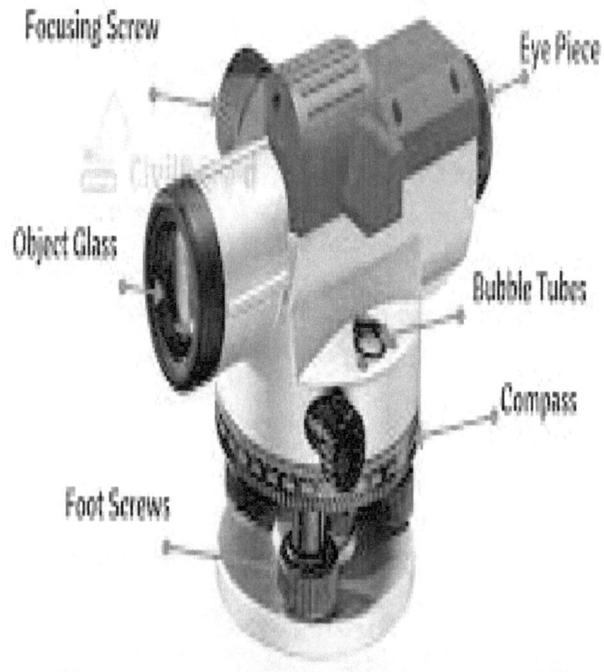

(3) **Digital electronic level:-** "A level staff" also called a leveling rod, is a graduated wooden or aluminum rod, the use of which permits the determination of differences in metric graduation as the left and imperial on the right leveling rods can be one piece, but many are sectional and can be shortened for storage and transport or lengthened for use. "Aluminum rods may adjust length by telescoping section inside each other, while wooden rod sections are attached to each other with sliding connections or slip joints. There are many types of rods, with names that identify the form of the graduations and other characteristics. Marking can be in imperial or metric units. Some rods are graduated on only one side while others are marked on both sides. If marked on both sides, the markings can be identical or, in some cases, can have imperial units on one side and metric on the other side".

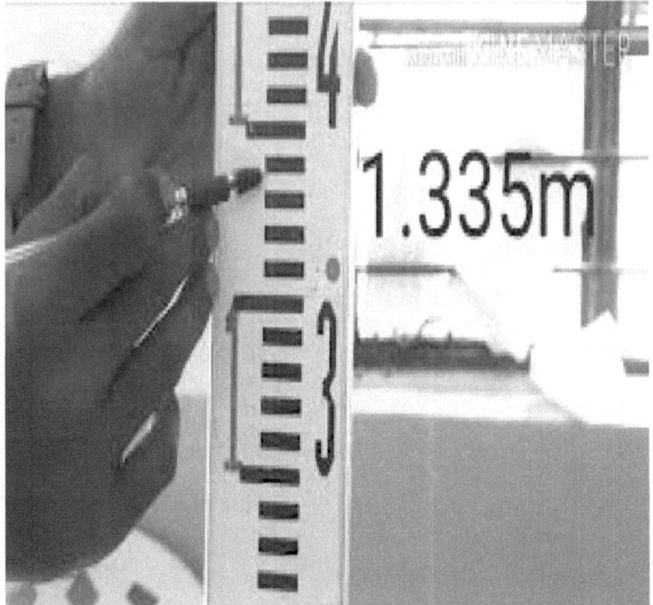

**The following are different steps to be follow in a temporary adjustment leveling:-**

**(1). Selection of suitable position:-** "A suitable location (point) is selected for setting the level. From this point," it should be possible to take the many number of observation without any difficulty and the ground should be fairly level".

**(2). Fixing level on tripod stand:-** "The tripod stand is placed at a required position with its legs well apart and press last into the ground. The level is fix on the top of the tripod stand according to the fixing arrangement provided for that particular level".

**(3). Approximate leveling by a leg on tripod stand:-** "The foot screw is brought to the centre of their run. Two legs of tripod stand are firmly fixed into the ground .then the third leg is moved right or left in or out until the bubble is approximately at the centre of its to run".

**(4). Perfect leveling by foot screw:-** As a perfect leveling the longitudinal bubble is on the top of the telescope the latter is placed parallel to any pair on foot screw. (i.e. $1^{st}$ position) and the bubble is brought to the centre by turning the foot screw equally either both inward and both outwards. "The telescope is then turned through $90^{0}$ and brought to a $3^{rd}$ foot screw and bubble is brought to be centre by turning this foot screw clockwise or anticlockwise the telescope again brought to its original position and the bubble is brought to centre".

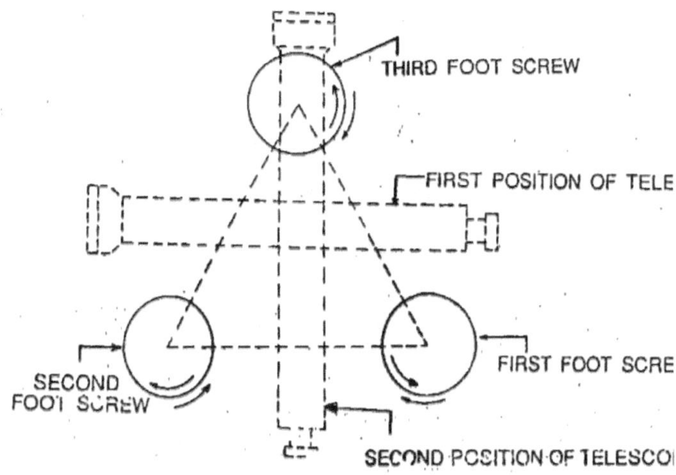


**(5).Focusing by eyepiece:-** A piece of white paper is held in front of the object glass and the eyepiece is moved in or out by turning it anticlockwise or clockwise until the cross hair can be seen firstly.

**(6). Focusing by object glass:-** "The telescope directed toward the leveling staff. Looking through the eyepiece the focusing screw is turned anticlockwise or clockwise until the graduation of the staff is distinctly visible & parallax is eliminated".

**(7). Taking staff reading:-** Finally the level of the instrument is verified by turning the telescope in any direction.

**Booking and Reducing Levels :-** There are two methods of booking and reducing the elevation of points from the observed staff reading:-

(1)  height of instrument or collimation method

(2) Rise and fall method

(1)       **height of instrument or collimation method:-** This method consist of finding height of instrument  for every setup of instrument; and after than obtaining the R.L. of point of reference with respect to height of instrument.

$$\text{CHECK LAST R.L- FIRST R.L} = \sum \text{B.S} - \sum \text{F.S}$$

**Example**

"The following staff readings were observed successively with a level the instrument is moved by third sixth and eighth readings.: 5.125 :4.325 :0.325 :3.175 :3.165 :5.215 0.825 :1.925 :1.125 :2.160 m enter the reading in record book and calculate R.L. if the first reading was taken at a B.M of 200.500 m".

| Station | B.S | I.S | F.S | HI | RL | REMARKS |
|---|---|---|---|---|---|---|
| 1 | 5.125 | | | 205.625 | 200.500 | B.M |
| 2 | | 4.325 | | | 201.300 | |
| 3 | 3.175 | | 0.325 | 208.475 | 205.300 | 3rd C.P |
| 4 | | 3.165 | | | 205.310 | |
| 5 | 0.825 | | 5.215 | 204.085 | 203.260 | 6th C.P |
| 6 | 1.125 | | 1.925 | 203.285 | 202.160 | 8th C.P |
| 7 | | | 2.160 | | 201.125 | |
| | 10.250 | | 9.625 | | | |

$$\text{CHECKLASTR.L-FIRSTR.L} = 201.125 - 200.500 = 0.625 = \sum \text{B.S} - \sum \text{F.S} = 10.250 - 9.625 = 0.625$$

(2)          **Rise and Fall method**:- It is the method of surveying to solve the leveling to find out the difference in elevation and elevation of two points. In this method like we need to calculate the difference in elevation of the staff of two points.

**CHECK $\sum$B.S – $\sum$F.S = $\sum$Rise – $\sum$Fall = Last R.L – First R.L**

**Example**

The following staff readings were observed successively with a level the instrument is moved by third sixth and eighth readings.: 5.225 :3.125 :0.125 :3.425 :2.125 :3.165: 0.825 :1.205 :2.125 :1.685 m enter the reading in record book and calculate R.L. if the first reading was taken at a B.M of 160.500 m

| Station | B.S | I.S | F.S | Rise | Fall | R.L | Remarks |
|---|---|---|---|---|---|---|---|
|  | 5.225 |  |  |  |  | 160.500 | B.M |
|  |  | 3.125 |  | 2.100 |  | 162.600 |  |
|  | 3.425 |  | 0.125 | 3.000 |  | 165.600 | 3rd C.P |
|  |  | 2.125 |  | 1.300 |  | 166.900 |  |
|  | 0.825 |  | 3.165 |  | 1.040 | 165.860 | 6th C.P |
|  | 2.125 |  | 1.205 |  | 0.380 | 165.480 | 8th C.P |
|  |  |  | 1.685 | 0.440 |  | 165.920 |  |
|  | 11.600 |  | 6.180 | 6.840 | 1.420 |  |  |

**CHECK LAST R.L- FIRST R.L= 165.920-160.500 =5.420=$\sum$B.S-$\sum$F.S=11.600-6.180 =5.420**

$=\sum$Rise-$\sum$Fall=6.840-1.420=5.420

**Conclusion:-**

In the field work, our group encountered errors in the results of the obtained data so we diagnosed the sources of error of leveling like inaccurate measurements of each reading on the rod at each point like error in instruments, human error, error in computation, and other errors. In order to lessen the error and improve the results of our field work next time, "I recommend that the precise level instrument should be checked if the lengths of the foresight and back sight are balanced by narrowing the collimator in order to adjust the movement in a correct direction, and also to adjust the focus of the image in measuring the back sight or foresight in order to reduce some refraction errors by avoiding blurred visualizations. I also recommend that in order to reduce errors, group should first analyze the situation of leveling, in which the set-up of the turning points and bench marks in leveling in this field work that has turning points on the low and high ground is quite different from the set-up for leveling from the previous fieldwork". After analyzing the situation of leveling, the group should make right choices in marking the intervening points between the bench marks in accordance with the manual. With this each surveyor should be given an opportunity to measure the values needed at each point.

**References:-**


- https://expertcivil.com/

- http://www.civildailyinfo.com/

- https://www.ebooksfree4u.com/2018/10/surveying-vol1-by-bc-punmia.html

- https://sbgstore.com/shop/north-surveying-vol-1-book-by-gs-bhatia/

## ANYONE CAN BE AN ENGINEER, "FLYING START, NO WINGS".

Author: Sapna Aggarwal
Assistant Professor
Department Of Computer Science and Engineering
Jind Institute of Engineering and Technology, Jind (126102), Haryana.

"Science can amuse and fascinate us all, but it is engineering that changes the world." "The engineer has been, and is, a maker of history." "Scientists study the world as it is; engineers create the world that has never been." **"The way to succeed is to double your failure rate."**

**An anonymous**

**Introduction: Why Engineer?**

Engineers are problem solvers. Engineers are innovators, who accept world's all challenges and find right path to improve our daily basic needs and lives. Their solutions & thoughts find right way to improve quality of lives.

So don't forget to remember some science quotes from some famous scientist about engineers, these quotes may motivate to spread roses in your path or may help to build some successful engineers.

"Engineers like to solve problems. If there are no problems handily available, they will create their own problems." — **Scott Adams**

This chapter provides a some points, how we can become an expert engineer. What is the basic requirement behind the life of a successful engineer? What are the key points which can motivate to everyone becomes an engineer. What ideas can give some wings to fly a normal people like a bird and give opportunities to touch the sky. This chapter represent how virtual perception is converted into real projects. So virtual perception or imagination are very important for building a successful engineer. There are some key points which help to understand how a normal person having a big aim can be converted to a real successful result.

So we can say

"Fly with your dreams, but don't fly in your dreams"

This quote is possible for everyone, but an engineering student can easily fulfil this dream.

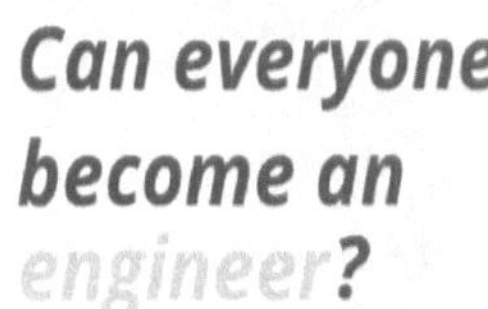

Figure:1

**Who is Engineer?**

An Engineer is a technical professional. An Engineer manage supervision of all tasks related to manufacturing, designing or as well as the process, production, development and manage all technical stuff. An Engineer is able to do research work on new techniques, he or she can invent new ideas, design new software, develop components of machine, construct new systems or can even design new system. With the help of team work, an engineer can manage all tasks very easily as comparison to other graduate students and try to innovate our society with new ideas.

A successful engineer can complete their project or work within given time and within budget.

Figure :2

This diagram defines the engineering design process. An engineer can image new innovative ideas, which is not possible for normal person and after thinking, he or she try to implement all ideas and convert a human virtual thought into real project.

- **"All knowledge that ends in words will die as quickly as it came to life, with the exception of the written word: which is its mechanical part" Leonardo da Vinci**

**Role of an engineer/ how we can successful Engineer**

I've chosen engineering as my career path because I believe Engineering is root to improve the technical environment.

1. **Decide your aim and make them happen**: Where to start and decide

Having aim for life and what we want to do, **is** an important part for career. So firstly decide, what to do, it can be a small thing or big thing; it's not matter of concern. Make proper planning for your goals and discuss with someone who can motivate and give wings to your goal. Firstly, think about small goals and then try to achieve your big aim. So proper planning is the main ingredient to find the final breakout and keep work hard so that we can find our final step.

2. **Promise yourself to continuous professional and technical development.**

To prove and enhance you, continuous professional is very important, so we can survive in technical environment. An engineer has required continuous professional and technical development due to rapid change in technical environment. Continuous professional development is ongoing process of developing, maintain and enhancing your skills according to latest trend of technical environment.

- There is no. of ways to improve your skills:

- Identify your requirements.

- Plan out development activities.

- Try both formal and informal learning.

- Reflecting on your learning.

- Try to share your new ideas and skills with others.

- Make Final Assessment (Final Development)

- Keep working on improve your problem solving skills

Problem solving skills or decision making is very important part in every field of management and engineering. So, every engineer has to keep work on developing your decision making and problem solving skills at each step in your career.

- It includes:-

- Active listening/ Good Listener

- Analysis and Research

- Creativity

- Decision Making

- Team building

This diagram represents:

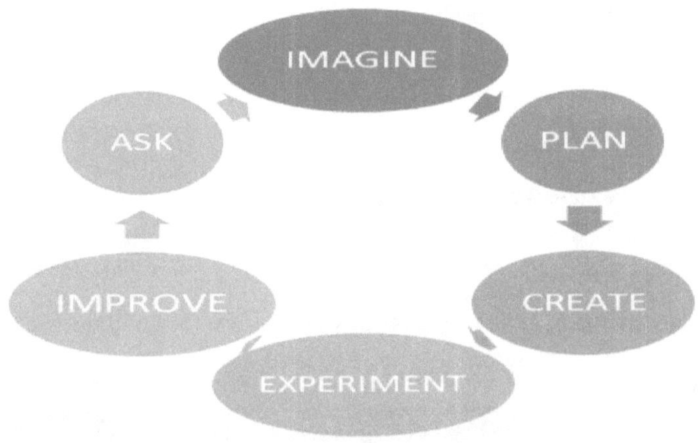


Figure: 3

First of all, define the problem, gather all information and generate all possible all solutions and then find all possible ideas and final evaluate the result.

### 3. Keep working on improve skills

Most of engineers, only focus on their professional and technical development. But it is very important to study the basics of soft skills like organization behaviour, team work, presentation skills and communication skills.

• Communication skills are main ingredient for successful career. In your professional career, you need to communicate with everyone at various stages. It is very important to develop your communication skills for all levels from juniors to seniors.

• Collaboration skills When we work together or in team work, and then we can solve problems very easily and at fast speed and find effective solution. So having good collaboration skills are very essential part for career.

4. **Try to learn from mistakes**

Mistakes are part of process. "Your last mistake is first teacher""I learn from my mistakes, it's very painful way to learn, but without pain, the old saying is, "there's no gain".

Figure: 4

- How we can learn from mistake, it includes:

- Indentify the mistake correctly.

- Understand your mistake.

- Learn to recover from mistakes.

- Make a review for the feedback of your mistake.

- Correct the mistake at the right time.

- Do self inspection.

### 5.  Understand Business

The people who make the decisions on the projects you work on will, more than likely, do so from a business perspective. As a result, they are more interested in return on investment than they are with the innovative approach you take to solving their problem. You don't have to become a businessperson, of course, but it helps if you understand what makes decision-makers tick.

It can also help to work with different business teams when the opportunity arises – teams outside engineering. This experience will help you better understand the different requirements and perspectives of the business. It will also help others in the company to better understand the perspectives of engineers.

### 6.  Embrace Change

Always be flexible, so you're ready to change. Due to rapid change in technology, it is very necessary to adopt changes so that an engineer can survive according to latest trends.

### 7.  Work Hard

Success is not an accident. It is matter or result of hard work. Preservance, learning, studying, sacrifice and most of all, are related to success.

**"Dream big, stay positive, work hard and enjoy the journey"**

8.  **Be Optimistic**

Optimism is a mindset that enables people to view the world in favourable and positive way. Optimism is like a mindset which represent how we can think positive in negative time.

"To the optimist, the glass is half full. To the pessimist, the glass is half empty. To the engineer, the glass is twice as big as it needs to be."
— **An anonymous**

There are some ways to be optimistic:-

- Focus on your success.

- Work hard.

- Focus on positive things

- Ignore negative things.

- Don't panic in difficult situation.

- Surround yourself with positive people.

- Try to keep happy yourself.

- Try to find solutions rather than keep focus on problems.

- Do not dwell on the past.

9.  **Focus on long Terms**

You can become a good engineer in short period of time, but real success can takes some time. You have to understand the difference between short term success and long term success just like difference between traders and investors in share markets. For long term success, we are investors.

Engineering require time, hard work, creativity, dedication, optimism and patience. Engineering is an exciting profession. So we can say, engineering requires:

- **Creativity**: It is perfect field for virtual and independent thinker.

- **You can mark your own presence**. Engineers are decision makers and problem solvers. Due to this great feature, engineer can mark your identity in technical world as well as in the nation.

- **You may get opportunity to work with passionate people**. Due to team work and collaboration skills, engineer can meet with different - different kind of people or mindset. So, Engineers will be surrounded by inspiring people or great personalities like architects, software developer, designers, doctors, and advocate and may be politician.

- **You'll never be bored**. Due to creativity nature of engineer, they try to evolve new ideas. With the help of new ideas and research on new task and technology, they always enhance your skills and meeting with different people always motivate you to stretch your talent in unexpected way.

- **Aim high, Big salary**. Engineers not only earn lots of fame and respect, but they also earn five to six digit salary per month without any financial investment. Even a fresher candidate can earn impressive salary.

•     **Enjoy job flexibility & opportunity to explore the world.** An engineer is a field, where an engineer can give wings to himself and fly like a bird anywhere. It means, an engineer have lots of opportunities to explore this beautiful world. An engineer can change the world.

*"Scientists investigate that which already is; engineers create that which has never been."*

*-Albert Einstein*

## ENGINEERING KNOWLEDGE OF ENGINEERS WITH SOCIETY.

Author: Sunita,

Assistant Professor,

Department of Computer Science and Engineering,

Jind Institute of Engineering and Technology, Jind (126102), Haryana.

### Who is engineer?

A person living on this mother earth (part of the world +part of the society) whose skills and knowledge comes to the society for use.

### What is engineer?

One who translate into action the dreams of humanity, traditional knowledge and concepts which based on science and technology to achieve management of society though the creative application of **"technology and science"**.

### What is necessary for human being (engineers)-knowledge?

As we move ahead in the $21^{st}$ century, in the knowledge base economy ,the need to upgrade our knowledge and skills to keep pace with the **'permanent white waters'** becomes all more important. However, the starting point should be the knowledge of oneself as a unique individual and how one relates to this new economy.

The ways of gaining knowledge are-

- **Self-awareness** – Self- awareness refers to your knowledge

and understanding of yourself, your emotions (your strengths and weakness, your likes and dislikes) Take time to discover your strengts by paying attention to the kind of work you do or you want to do, what kind of work do you feel energized to work on, what do others comment on the quality of your work, what type of projects are you naturally drawn toward.

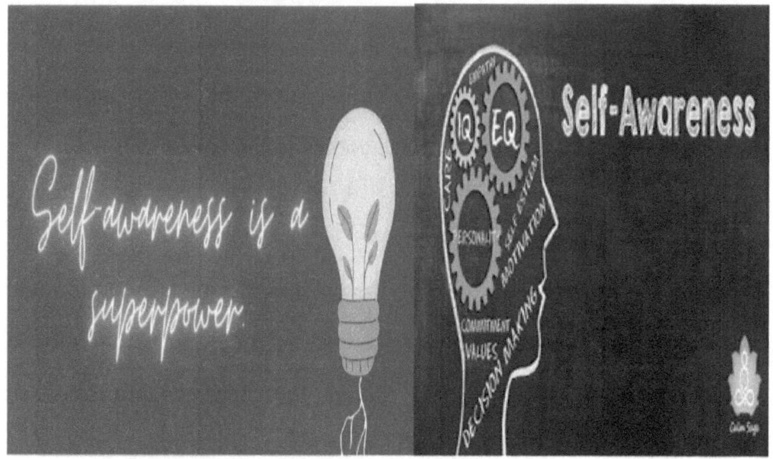


And as you discover your weakness you either learn them yourself **Or** be Humble enough to ask for friends or family or Someone else's support (someone else's support is very difficult in this **KALYUG** but you remain humble may be because of **GOD** someone helps you and it is also right said that '**God helps those, who helps themselves).**

**Also** via Self-motivation (ability to identify effective method of getting yourself to move from thoughts to action) **and** via Self-regulation (a systematic efforts allow you to keep a tab on your own emotions resulting as your response to a specific event and attune your actions accordingly to accomplish your set goal) you become a Self-Aware person.

Self-aware towards the attainment of one's goal has assumed great importance in the Psychological and Educational Literatures.

• Communication skills- this allows us to express our needs, wants and other things to other human Or animals.

Human communicate with others via different medium-

• Vocally[Using voice(Via using some language - a language is a syntactically organized system of signals, such as voice sounds, intonations or pitch, gestures) which help in communicating our thoughts, feelings, ideas]

• Written [Using printed or digital media such as magazines, websites or emails, Books (As we are communicating with each other)].

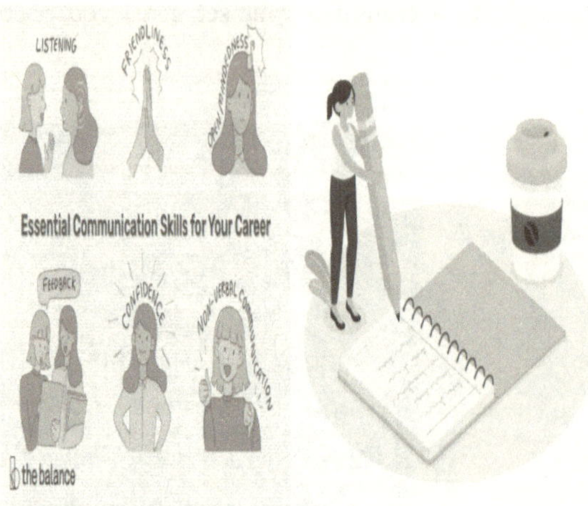

- **V**isually (Using logos, maps, charts or graphs).

Whatever be the medium, Communication Still Means that some message is being transferred from one source (Sender of the message) to the chosen target (Receiver of the message) or in the same way in the Computing Environment communication held between Client-Server.

Communication also carried out between machines or parts of machines or machine-to-

Machine [As in IOT devices (Smart Home, Smart Doors etc.)].

**W**hen you are General Aware and having Domain Knowledge Only then you can Communicate-

• General-Awareness (About your Surroundings including latest events of the world around you. It gives you the confidence to communicate with Conviction).

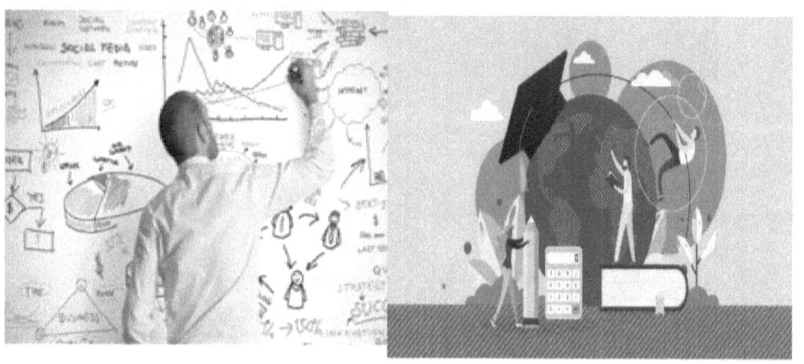

• Domain Knowledge (Your expertise in your chosen area- Arts, Commerce, Science etc. Being well informed about the latest happenings helps you to communicate with Confidence).

You must a Good Listener because it is a key component of our learning process.

**NOW** a Person Equipped with Self Skills and Knowledge are ready for the Society TO Use And this person also must have the Capabilities (Which are Necessity of day to day Professional as well as Personal Life).

• Multitasking

• Organizational Skills (Essential requirement to know what to do, When and Where to Start and When to Finish Everything on Time).

• Discipline (To keep you and your action in track for the Successful completion of the task at hand).

• Negotiating Skills (It is your ability to see the big picture. It calls for Foresightedness and Willingness to accommodate others' ideas for the benefit of all).

• Flexibility or Adaptability [It's your quality to adapt your Working style (Without compromising with the Quality of work) to suit other people working with you].

• Ability to deal with **Rejection** and not to take it Personally- This calls for a 'Never-Say-Die' Attitude and open-mindedness to face failure and yet not get Disheartened and start a fresh with new Innovative thoughts.

Now you or a Person or an Engineer has adapted Enough Skills to seek out a particular Problem or to invent a new Technology for the betterment of your surroundings.

To further sought a problem or to invent, you first gather information (feasibility study), Make a Planning for solution, (Analyze, Design, Development, Testing, Implementation and Maintain them), and give that invented or developed Technology to the Society.    BUT, that techno should be based on **SUSTAINABLE RESOURCES OR SUSTAINABLE DEVELOPMENT SKILLS** i.e. involving the use of Natural Products and Energy in a way that does not harm the Environment.

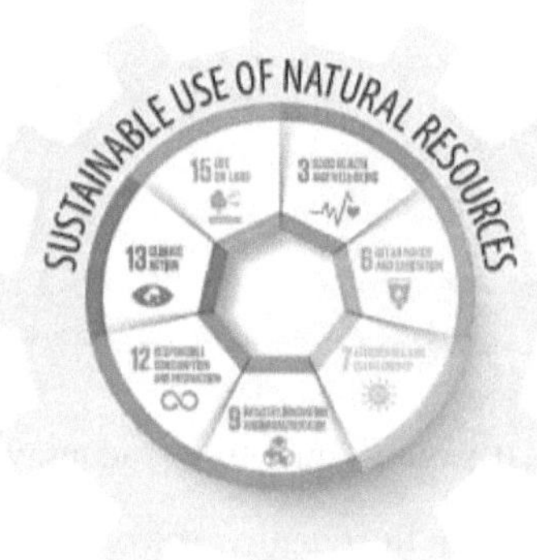

**Now the Question arise is this new Techno doing Good to Nature and Society?**

**If they are acting in a Good way then-**

You can become like a **Civil Engineer Sir Ganga Ram Ji,** Who just in age of 70 years was able to invent electricity from water falling from near 6 feet.

He Astound the whole world and earned a Great Fame and Respectable position (By providing the provision of water He converted the Barren land into Fertile Soil).

His Motive was to work for benefit of Human and Nature.

**And in another example Allen Musk**(Who became Rocket Scientist from Software Engineer)-  Send human for the first time to Space through his company Space-x and also Envision to send Human beings to marsh.

**If** Acting **in a bad way-**

Then in a Rat Race of being Superior one can become like China (For the reason), who has Shattered the Economy And Education of the Whole World Since last Three Years.

**So Free Yourself from This Rat Race and Become Like**

**Sir Gang Ram Ji.**

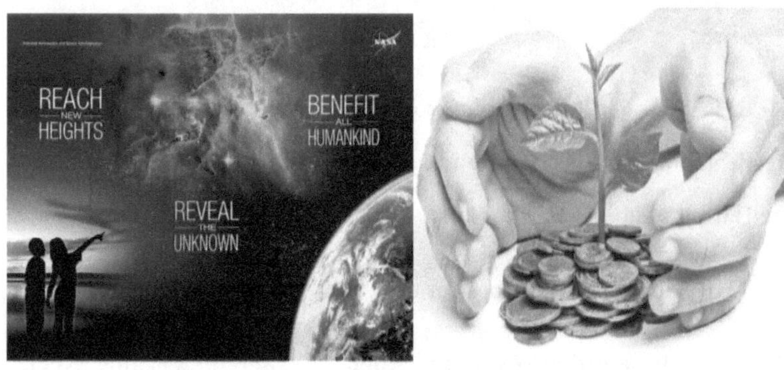


**AND Importantly Keep Welfare Oriented Intentions for Mankind THEN There will be nothing left that this HUMAN WORLD can not Conquer.**